THE PR MASTERCLASS

THE PR MASTERCLASS

ALEX SINGLETON

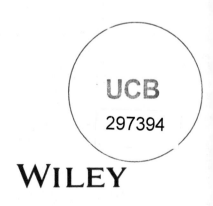

WILEY

Registered office

John Wiley and Sons Ltd, The Atrium, Southern Gate, Chichester, West Sussex, PO19 8SQ, United Kingdom

For details of our global editorial offices, for customer services and for information about how to apply for permission to reuse the copyright material in this book please see our website at www.wiley.com.

The right of the author to be identified as the author of this work has been asserted in accordance with the Copyright, Designs and Patents Act 1988.

Reprinted May 2015, October 2015

Library of Congress Cataloging-in-Publication Data is available

A catalogue record for this book is available from the British Library.

ISBN 978-1-118-75623-2 (hardback)   ISBN 978-1-118-75620-1 (ebk)
ISBN 978-1-118-75619-5 (ebk)

Cover design by Jason Anscomb

Set in 10.5/16 pt PalatinoLTStd by Toppan Best-set Premedia Limited

Printed in the UK

CONTENTS

FOREWORD

By Francis Ingham
Director General of the Public Relations Consultants Association
Visiting Professor in Public Relations at the University of Westminster

Crudely speaking, there are two types of books on PR, carrying with them two types of uses. The first type is the pseudo-academic book, probably written by somebody with little or no knowledge of PR. You've probably never heard of the author. That book's primary use is to light your fire, line your cat's litter tray or prop open a door. Good trees died in vain so that it might live.

The second book is by somebody who actually understands PR, because they work in it. That book has a completely different use – it's there to educate, guide and inform. It is a good thing. You should read it.

I'm delighted to say that Alex Singleton's book is most definitely in the latter category – which is why I'm delighted to be writing its foreword.

Ours is a vibrant, growing industry. It informs and inspires the majority of what you hear about from the media. And, in so doing, it moulds choices, opinions and visions. Because of that fact, it plays a fundamental role in shaping our world. Obviously, that role can be for good or for ill. But its power is undeniable.

Yet it is also an industry of contrasts. The majority of practitioners in our industry are not members of professional bodies, and probably aren't eligible to be so. The code of conduct that distinguishes PRCA members from the others, for example, is valuable not least because of the contrast it draws between those willing and able to subscribe to rules and sanctions – and those who are neither willing nor able.

Our industry prides itself on professional skills and relationship building, yet all too often fails to invest in either. For a trade of such power, we spend remarkably little time focused on honing the power we exercise. That needs to change.

Our industry all too often strives after the ephemeral and intangible at the expense of the important. Its biggest failure is a propensity to – how should I put it? – be rather up itself. That is, to fail to see the reality of our craft, rather than somebody's artificial representation of it.

This book falls into none of those traps. It is practical, direct, correct and insightful. It recognises, for example, that we should of course talk about how digital is changing our industry. And we absolutely must explain why PR should have a strategic as well as a tactical function. And, for that matter, why reputation management is vital.

But it recognises that the bread and butter of PR continues to be about relationships with journalists, colleagues and clients. Good writing skills; the ability to spell (all too often lacking in new recruits to our industry); a capacity not just to tolerate the company of clients and journalists, but actually to enjoy it; and the ability instinctively to see the angle and to know the nascent story – all of these remain vital to PR.

It's all too easy to lose sight of these basic facts. I have sat through dozens of talks about Grunig,[1] and new paradigms, and symbiotic relationships, and all of that stuff. It all has a place, and I do genuinely respect that place. But it is far from the being the entirety – or indeed the mainstay – of our industry. And sometimes when people seek so very, very hard to create an artificial intellectual construct with which they can frame our industry's work, they serve only to obscure what it does, and to confuse us all.

The glory of this book is that it doesn't make any of those mistakes. And there is an obvious reason why not. It is written by a poacher-turned-gamekeeper – by a former and respected journalist who moved to PR. Because of that background, he knows what journalists are looking for. He knows the things that annoy them – like calling on deadline "just to check you received our release". Like poorly written copy. Like spamming journos. Like failing to realise that the journalists' role isn't to serve your clients' interests. All of that insight is of incredible value.

Over the past few years, our industry has grown considerably. It has done so despite the strongest economic headwinds in living memory. It is a career of choice, offering good pay, intelligent colleagues and excellent prospects. And if that is true of the UK, it is even more valid outside of it. A recent magazine front cover described how "spin doctors" were taking over the world. Its language was rather over the top, and its term of choice – spin doctor – was an unfortunate throwback to a time when our

---

[1] "The Importance of the Four Models of Public Relations", http://iml.jou.ufl.edu/projects/fall99/westbrook/models.htm (accessed March 4, 2013)

industry foolishly embraced that sobriquet. But the message was clear and right – that ours in an industry of the future.

But every industry of the future needs a route map for its practitioners. Otherwise, they're likely to get lost. And that is why I welcome wholeheartedly this book – an accurate, accessible and powerful atlas for anyone seeking their way through the PR jungle.

PREFACE

There is a golden rule in media relations, but one that most people forget. Give journalists what they want. And what do journalists want? Well, more money mostly – but offering that would be unethical. What they actually need from you are story ideas that *interest* their readers.

If you provide this effectively, you get a lot of coverage. But, until now, it has been difficult to find practical information on how to do this well. This book, for the first time, gives an insider's view on getting press coverage.

I started writing for newsstand consumer magazines in 1994, was a staff journalist at *The Daily Telegraph* and *Sunday Telegraph*, and have also written for *The Guardian*, the *Daily Express*, *CityAM* and, online, for the *Daily Mail*. Intermingled with that press experience, I have also worked trying to secure coverage in the media – and I've lived and worked in three countries: the United Kingdom, the United States and Belgium. In this book I'd like to share with you what I learned from all the mistakes, experiments and successes I've made along the way.

These days I have a pretty accurate gut instinct of what will get good coverage. But this was not always the case – and it is difficult to acquire. Rarely do journalists properly explain their thinking. They say: "I'm sorry but there wasn't space." This, I'm afraid, just means the proposal wasn't good enough. After all, if it had been brilliant, they would have made space. Other journalists avoid these conversations. They recognise an unwanted PR pitch from the caller display and just don't pick up the phone.

What I've realised is that, despite the impression some people have that public relations is easy, there's actually a huge amount to learn. That is why, in this book, you'll occasionally hear me bemoaning the failure of some PR practitioners to grow their skills. Despite lots of media experience, it was only when actually I joined the staff of a national newspaper that I was able to soak up what people at the very top of the journalistic trade really thought about PR pitches. The experience radically transformed my understanding of what is newsworthy and what is not.

A note about terminology

This book focuses on media relations. Public relations is undoubtedly broader than just trying to generate media coverage – including everything from event management, to internal staff communications, to advising executives on what to say to regulators. But it is worth noting the central position that Trevor Morris and Simon Goldsworthy (who lecture in public relations at the University of Westminster) give to media coverage within public relations. They describe PR as: "the planned persuasion of people to behave in ways that further its sponsor's objectives. It works primarily through the use of media relations and other forms of third party endorsement."[2]

---

[2] Trevor Morris and Simon Goldsworthy, *PR: A Persuasive Industry? Spin, Public Relations and the Shaping of the Modern Media* (London: Palgrave Macmillan, 2008), p. 102.

Some in the PR industry would prefer a definition that saw PR as giving strategic, board-level advice to the biggest listed companies. But that is to confuse what the most senior practitioners are doing with the majority of the work. Indeed, it's a bit like saying house-building is about structural engineering and is nothing to do with brick-laying or plumbing. As Morris and Goldsworthy go on to say: "Few modern PR campaigns lack a media element and most have media coverage at their heart. Indeed, the PR industry's reluctance to admit to the centrality of media relations . . . flies in the face of the understanding of PR in wider society. To most outsiders PR is forever, and overwhelmingly, associated with journalism and the media."[3]

Anyway, I tried to imagine what a normal person sitting in front of Amazon's search function would think to look for. It struck me that the target audience for this book would almost exclusively say that they need something on "public relations".

This concurred with my experience hosting workshops teaching similar sessions, in which I found that internet users searching for "media training" were really executives nervous about imminent television appearances, while "PR training" was used by people wanting to sell products or ideas through the press.

Why conventional media still matters

Some people – especially, I'm afraid to say, those who are unskilled at securing press coverage – assert that the conventional media no longer matters. What is important, they claim, is social media

---

[3] Ibid, p. 105.

– sites like Twitter and Facebook. And, for sure, engaging with social media is an important part of public relations. But these people are wrong if they believe that the conventional media is dead. What is actually happening is that much of it – especially the trade press and daily news – is moving online. That is not death: it is a change of format.

Many of the conventional media publications have transformed, or are in the process of changing, into hugely popular destinations online. Newspapers such as the *Daily Mail*, *The Guardian* and *The New York Times* now have a global readership that, on a daily basis, dwarfs what they ever achieved in print. Martin Clarke, the publisher of the *Daily Mail*'s website, says of his site: "People are addicted to it. It's like journalism crack."[4] Meanwhile, there are no signs that viewers are rejecting quality broadcasters. The BBC's global audience hit 239 million people a week in 2012, up 6 per cent from the previous year.[5] And it is worth noting what happened during the mindless riots in the UK in August 2011. Social media was given credit both for helping rioters to mobilise[6] and also for assisting community minded citizens to clear up the damage.[7] But when the public wanted authoritatively to know what was happening, conventional media played a massive role. On August 9, 13.1 million people turned to the BBC News Channel, while a 10pm bulletin on BBC

---

[4] http://www.mediaweek.co.uk/news/1174031/Mail-Online-journalism-crack -says-editor/ (accessed March 12, 2013).

[5] http://www.bbc.co.uk/blogs/theeditors/2012/06/new_audience_figures _for_bbc_g.html (accessed March 8, 2013).

[6] http://www.guardian.co.uk/media/2011/nov/08/two-thirds-support-social -media-blackout (accessed March 8, 2013).

[7] http://www.huffingtonpost.co.uk/2011/12/08/twitter-did-not-incite-uk -riots_n_1136306.html (accessed March 8, 2013).

One got 7.6 million viewers. ITV's *News at Ten* was watched by 2.9 million people, and in one 15-minute segment Sky News pulled in 9.28 million. So much for the death of the conventional media.

Two things have changed. First, some of the barriers to entry have been removed. Expensive printing presses are not necessary for web publishing. YouTube lets anyone with a smartphone record and share footage, and give their own video reports of the news.

Second, the media is globalising. That is particularly savage for American city newspapers which once practically had local monopolies. They now find their readers logging on to read not just internet-only news sites, such as *The Huffington Post*, but also to what the British, Irish, Australian and New Zealand media think.

Television stations in the UK now face competition from the heavily resourced American-owned Netflix internet service, which spent $100 million on the hit TV show *House of Cards*.[8] And the BBC – ITN duopoly on national and international TV news was shattered, first with introduction of Sky News (major shareholder: News Corporation, headquartered in New York), then with cable and satellite services beaming in countless international news programmes (from France 24 to Al Jazeera), and now with the commonplace use of video on news websites.

Does this increased competition mean that the conventional media is doomed? Well, not in my view. It is clearly painful to

---

[8] http://money.cnn.com/2013/02/01/technology/innovation/netflix-house -of-cards/index.html (accessed March 8, 2013).

many media companies. Many more will go to the wall. But there will still be mass media, and – contrary to the doom-filled whining of some – plenty of it will be high quality.

You see, there are lots of markets where the barriers to entry seem low, but where some of the big players have huge market shares. Anyone can make a cup of coffee, yet consumers flock to brands such as Starbucks. In 2012, the global coffee giant turned over $13.3 billion and traded in 61 countries.[9] Professor Priya Raghubir of New York University's Stern School of Business talks of "the enduring brand loyalty" of the chain. "Starbucks stands for coffee; it's converted that into an experience . . . I think they [the customers] value the convenience, they value the welcome, they value the fact that they can find the Starbucks anywhere . . . and offerings are uniform."[10] In other words, using Starbucks is extremely reliable – and this is information its brand communicates to us.

Similarly, anyone can broadcast news over the internet, but not everyone has a strong news brand. In war, in particular, I don't just want to watch five-second YouTube clips that supposedly show one side behaving badly, or to merely read a view expressed in 140 characters on Twitter. I rely upon brands such as the BBC or CNN to bring a researched perspective that I trust.

Moreover, the boundaries between the conventional media and social media have blurred. Blogs, once regarded as a rival to

---

[9]Starbucks 2012 Annual Report, http://investor.starbucks.com/phoenix .zhtml?c=99518&p=irol-reportsAnnual (accessed March 12, 2013).
[10] http://www.huffingtonpost.com/2013/03/07/starbucks-brand -loyalty_n_2830372.html (accessed March 12, 2013).

big media, have been adopted wholeheartedly by newspaper and magazine websites, from *The Atlantic* to *The Telegraph*. Nowadays, reader comments at the bottom of articles are providing writers with instant feedback, while Twitter – with its messages limited to 140 characters – is inevitably pointing us in the direction of worthwhile journalism, wherever it appears in the world. In 2010 the *Daily Mail* revealed that 10 per cent of its UK traffic came from Facebook. Martin Clarke, publisher of the *Daily Mail*'s website, said that: "Facebook isn't a threat or a parasite but a gigantic free marketing engine."

The biggest stars of the blogosphere also became stars of the conventional media: Guido Fawkes, a political gossip blogger, got a column in Rupert Murdoch's *Sun* newspaper, Tim Montgomerie, who launched the ConservativeHome blog, became Comment Editor of *The Times* and Iain Dale, who was one of Britain's earliest political bloggers, became a top radio presenter. On the BBC's *Question Time* programme, it has almost become an integrated part of the show that viewers tweet their views of the show's guests and the annoyingness of the studio audience. And finally, when ITV News announced a relaunch of its website in 2012,[11] it started displaying stories in a "live stream", with older stories flowing down the page, just as you would expect on Twitter.

As I see it, the written and broadcast media is principally about *content*, while social media is principally about *contact* (that is to say, the online interaction with others we like). In fact, social media's other name, social networking, is often more apt. Both

---

[11] http://madebymany.com/blog/striding-with-itv-into-the-future-of-news (accessed November 19, 2013).

types of media are useful. But those who pretend that the conventional media no longer counts are promoting a fantasy, which is not borne out by the readership and viewer figures. After all, the invention of the telephone – an early social network – didn't stop people wanting to read journalism. Neither will social media.

And with that out of the way, let's get started.

Chapter 1

Why Public Relations Campaigns Fail – and How to Make Them Succeed

Have you ever seen a hippopotamus? Quite often, you will find that they have a bird on their back. It's a friendship that benefits both sides. The hippo isn't able to reach to clean its back. Yet potentially harmful parasites embed themselves up there. So the hippo makes friends with certain types of bird, who get to feast on the parasites. Both sides benefit.

Good media relations is like that two-way friendship. The effective PR person is always thinking: what is in the interests of the journalist? The ineffective PR person only asks: what message does my employer want me to drum repeatedly?

Alas, the vast majority of PR pitches – even from some big PR agencies – fail to acknowledge the needs of journalists.

Ignorance isn't bliss

The simple and most effective investment you can make in your public relations is to buy and read the publications that you want to get coverage in. I know that sounds obvious – much of what you will read in this book is, on one level, common sense. Yet it is rarely followed. I often come across people who complain, for example, that they cannot get newspapers or magazines to cover their material – but who do not have any copies of those publications in their offices. Of course, they may be accessing them on their tablets, but invariably they are not.

PR is like other forms of marketing: too many of the people doing it are clueless. According to Professors Morris and Goldsworthy, a survey they conducted with one of the largest PR firms "found that few if any employees recalled reading any books about PR".[12] That is good – for you. It means that with the basics you will learn in this book, you can outperform many of your rivals. I frequently find even sizable companies – turning over more than £100m a year – who run appallingly unsuccessful PR campaigns, despite employing supposedly well-qualified in-house people to run them. Those staff just haven't invested time to develop their skills.

The truth is that for all the PR industry's claims of professionalism, too much of what gets done in its name is based on ignorance. Of the 60,000 people in full-time PR jobs in the United Kingdom, perhaps 15,000 are highly skilled. Only they do things like going on training courses and reading books to keep their skills sharp, and join the Public Relations Consultants Association and read *CorpComms* to keep up to date with best practice.

In the United States, the Bureau of Labor Statistics estimates that there are 212,510 public relations specialists,[13] the vast majority of whom are not members of a professional body or trade

---

[12] Trevor Morris and Simon Goldsworthy, *PR Today: The Authoritative Guide to Public Relations* (London: Palgrave Macmillan, 2011), p. 25.

[13] Bureau of Labor Statistics Economic News Release, http://www.bls.gov/news.release/ocwage.t01.htm (accessed February 25, 2013).

association. If there is a similar split between skilled and unskilled practitioners as in the UK, that would mean around 160,000 of American PR practitioners need to radically improve their skills.

This problem is not new. Edward Bernays, one of the founders of modern public relations, told *The New York Times* in 1991 that "Public relations today is horrible. Any dope, any nitwit, any idiot can call him or herself a public relations practitioner." They give the industry a bad name.

That so much PR is bad means that there is no reason why even small companies – with decent PR – cannot propel themselves into the limelight. Indeed, many firms have been built from scratch using PR as the biggest tool in their marketing arsenals.

But no PR programme will be truly successful unless it is based on a genuine understanding of the worldview and the sort of articles publications prefer. Edward Bernays, writing in 1923, defined an important duty of the public relations practitioner:

> The public relations counsel is first and foremost a student. His field of study is the public mind. His text books for this study are the facts of life; the articles printed in newspapers and magazines, the advertisements that are inserted in publications, the billboards that line the streets, the railroads and the highways, the speeches that are delivered in legislative chambers, the sermons issuing from pulpits, anecdotes related in smoking rooms, the gossip of Wall Street, the patter of the theatre and the conversation of the other men who, like them, are interpreters and must listen for the clear or obscure enunciations of the public.[14]

---

[14] Bernays, Edward L., *Crystallizing Public Opinion* (New York: IG Publishing, 1923) p. 78.

The so-called "low information diet", popularised by Tim Ferriss,[15] who suggests that we should stop reading the news, isn't an option for those wanting to do well in public relations. Practitioners who are not reading to develop their general knowledge just won't prosper. Titles such as *The Economist*, *Bloomberg BusinessWeek*, *Wired* and, of course, the newspapers are useful mind fodder.

How to get started

It doesn't matter what sort of media outlet you're interested in: you need to read the publication religiously. That might mean decamping to a major city library for a few days and reading the back issues. It certainly should mean getting a subscription, if it's a print publication, or always picking up a copy from the newsstand. Only if you engross yourself in a publication will you truly understand what to pitch to its journalists.

Let's say you are trying to get coverage for a startup business manufacturing camera bags, of various designs. The first thing to do is to walk into a big newsagent and buy all the titles about photography – there are lots of them.

You can find out which titles are the most important from looking at their audited circulation figures. The International Federation of Audit Bureaux of Circulations has member bureaux that create reliable figures for how many people read each major publication. These bureaux cover the circulations of titles in forty countries, although there are some agencies that are independent of the global federation. You can find out more at www.ifabc.org,

---

[15] Tim Ferriss, *The 4-Hour Work Week* (London: Vermilion, 2011), p. 10.

where you can click through to an agency in your country. Some of the major circulation bureaux are:

- United Kingdom and Ireland   www.abc.org.uk
- United States   www.auditedmedia.com
- Canada   www.auditedmedia.ca
- Australia   www.auditbureau.org.au
- New Zealand   www.abc.org.nz
- The Netherlands   www.hoi-online.nl
- Denmark   www.do.dk
- Sweden   www.ts.se

Given that your time is likely to be limited, it makes sense to concentrate on publications that (a) are instinctively most interested in your work and (b) have the highest circulations.

For an online publication, you can work out how popular it is using a website called alexa.com, which displays how well-read the site is relative to others. Many major news sites now have their online readers audited by the Audit Bureaux of Circulations.

Looking at the circulation figures can be eye-opening. In the UK, there are local papers that outsell national ones. As I type this, the circulation figures for the *Liverpool Echo* show that it outsells *The Independent* – just. And the *London Evening Standard*, despite being a local newspaper, is one of the most-read papers in the land. I am sure that a lot of PR campaigns ignore local papers as unimportant – but I say look at the circulation figures before making that sort of judgement. Similarly, there are blogs which have a bigger readership than mainstream publications. Is there anything more widely read in the Westminster political world than the gossip-filled *Guido Fawkes Blog*? Everyone in UK politics seems to read the site, even if they hate it. Meanwhile, *The Daily Caller*, which was founded in 2010 and is only available online, breaks major stories and is one of Washington DC's most important news outlets.

As – in our example – you're making camera bags, let's say you are interested in *Amateur Photographer*, one of the most-read photography publications, which has been going since 1884. By reading the news pages over several issues, you discover that its news editor is interested in bossy police officers and security guards who pretend that they have legal powers to stop photographers taking photos in public places. You see, amateur photographers often set up tripods in public places to take chocolate-box images of famous buildings. And some security people think this is suspicious. ("Why is he taking photographs? He must be a terrorist!")

Armed with this knowledge, you produce a free booklet about the legal aspects of photography in public places. The idea is that photographers can store it in their camera bag and show it to the police, if challenged.

You contact the news editor of *Amateur Photographer* and tell him that you will post this free guide to anyone who requests it from your website. You get to build up a mailing list of keen photographers, the public gets a useful guide, and the magazine gets a news story.

However, this story would be completely irrelevant to *Outdoor Photography* magazine. Its readers are landscape photographers predominantly taking shots in the countryside, and therefore are unlikely to be stopped by the police.

The dreary product or personnel announcement

There is only one thing a journalist finds more boring than a press release announcing a new product. It is a press release announcing a personnel change. If that's what your firm is doing currently, I hope this book – especially the next chapter – will show you a better path.

Admittedly, the press releases just mentioned do sometimes work – and can actually be a mainstay of trade publications. The appointment of a new CEO at a major industry player will normally cause a story with a photograph to appear in a trade publication, while a more junior appointment might get an inch somewhere in an "in brief" column. However, they won't play so well, if at all, in consumer titles. Yes, when Apple launches a new product or changes its CEO, consumer news organisations are desperate to cover it. But most people doing PR aren't lucky enough to be representing Apple, and most such announcements aren't jumped upon by the press.

The reality is that the vast majority of press releases – perhaps 95 per cent – are ignored by the media. Yet, amazingly, even many big companies are still totally reliant on product and personnel press releases, which is why their media coverage is far less than their size of business deserves. There are PR teams – ones that don't read books like this – who are paid good money, but day-in, day-out issue press releases that are simple, boring announcements. They get some coverage – but not much.

If you want to generate sizeable coverage, your PR has to be at a higher level.

What higher-level PR looks like

Andrew Gadsden is an entrepreneur who blends tea in a factory in Portsmouth, near England's best-known naval port. Although he sells hundreds of teas, his main product is Portsmouth Tea, which is a better quality of tea than that sold in supermarkets, giving a fuller flavour. He has built up a strong reputation in the city and people have started to buy Portsmouth Tea, over the internet, from all over the country.

Instead of simply issuing press releases saying that he is selling tea, he does things that the media genuinely finds interesting. One endeavour was to beat a world record: he created the world's largest teabag and unveiled it on board the HMS *Warrior*, which is moored at Portsmouth.

This simple, relatively low-cost activity secured him an interview on the ITV local television news, a story on the BBC News website and lots of local coverage. I have linked to the coverage at www.alexsingleton.com/teabag.

As a result of the coverage, he's able to show current and prospective customers that his company has been featured on the biggest British TV networks, the BBC and ITV. Although the articles and news reports generated are not product reviews, the public still sees them as third-party endorsements. Or, to use the clichéd, but remarkably effective, phrase, his company, AllAboutTea.co.uk, is "as seen on TV". If the BBC and ITV think Portsmouth Tea is kosher enough to cover, it must be decent.

But it is hardly surprising that Andrew's company gets coverage. When I visited his factory, he picked up a newspaper – one of those things rarely on display in bad PR agencies – and started explaining what he liked about it. If you know your publications, you'll do well.

How to capture the results of good PR

Some of the people who see your company's name in print or on the television will search for your website. However, they will not necessarily, at that very moment, be ready to buy from you. It is vital that you set up your website to capture their email addresses before they forget who you are.

Just as with journalists, you need to offer people something interesting in return. Andrew Gadsden, for example, offers a free tea course, in which people learn by email about the varied types of tea he sells. People will be far more likely to give you their email address if they think they will get something valuable in return, rather than just advertising emails.

For best results, avoid sending out emails that look like glossy leaflets, and instead focus on talking with your prospects as though you were sending an email just to them. Many people's email software is set to block images. And there are still people who will read them on some primitive BlackBerry phone. Drayton Bird, who has spent a lifetime measuring the responses to marketing and built the UK's largest direct marketing agency, says that: "E-mails that look like text almost always outperform ones with pretty pictures".[16]

---

[16] Drayton Bird, "31 Insiders' Direct Marketing Ploys", http://draytonbird commonsense.com/sites/default/files/e-books/DraytonBird_31Ploys_priceless .pdf (accessed February 23, 2013).

The best way to cope with people subscribing and unsubscribing is to use one of the popular services that automates the management of the list. Good tools to manage email lists leapfrog each other, but at the time of writing I like both Aweber and GetResponse. They are easy to use and free people up from the complexity of installing and then upgrading email list software on their own webservers. Usefully, both of these tools let you write pre-written emails that get sent to subscribers according to a predetermined schedule. That means all new subscribers get, for example, a follow-up email exactly a week after subscribing.

I maintain a list of good mailing list tools at www.alexsingleton.com/emailers (which I update as the technology progresses).

The need to measure PR

Ninety years ago Claude Hopkins wrote *Scientific Advertising*. This showed that by measuring the sales resulting from particular advertisements, bad ads could be ditched and the best techniques learned.

PR practitioners, however, are only just catching up. In his American book on measurement,[17] Mark Weiner says that the PR industry has lagged behind because of "loosely defined professional standards, generally inadequate levels of professional education and talent development, and the self-perpetuation of the myth that PR can't be measured scientifically". Ouch.

---

[17] Mark Weiner, *Unleashing the Power of PR: A Contrarian's Guide to Marketing and Communication* (San Franciso: Jossey-Bass, 2006), p. 21.

Actually, there are many difficulties with measuring PR – just as in any social science. But none are sufficient to justify pursuing PR without modern evaluation.

When I was first a press officer in the 1990s, we measured in a simple way – we counted the number of press cuttings. Twice a week the International Press-Cutting Bureau would send us our clippings and we would glue them in a book. Measuring this way may have been basic, but it was a cheap and effective way of assessing our effectiveness. We would then analyse the coverage qualitatively.

Counting the cuttings is still an objective, basic method that startups and small businesses can use easily – though it does have a downside. Funders of PR campaigns just can't tell from a cuttings book if the coverage is genuinely achieving business goals, or merely acting as a vanity exercise. Yet it remains commonplace. A 2003 survey conducted in the United States by *PR News* found that 84 per cent of respondents used clip-counting as their primary measure of success.[18]

Until recently, a measurement called Advertising Value Equivalency (AVE) was popular among those wanting a more sophisticated approach. Actually it still is commonplace, despite (justifiably) irritating the PR chatterati. The AVE calculates what the column inches would have cost to buy as advertising. It is a problematic method because an advert says exactly what you want it to say, whereas editorial does not. That doesn't stop users

---

[18] "Exploring the Link Between Volume of Media Coverage and Business Outcomes", Institute for PR, 2006, http://www.instituteforpr.org/iprwp/wp-content/uploads/Media_Coverage_Business06.pdf (accessed February 24, 2013).

of AVEs then multiplying the figure by anything from two to ten times – but most commonly by three – on the grounds that editorial coverage is more convincing than advertising.

Professor Tom Watson, in a paper presented to the International History of Public Relations conference in 2012, wrote about a study of 500 PR practitioners. It found that AVEs "were the third most popular measurement method for judgment of communication effectiveness, after clippings counts and internal reviews, and the first amongst methods of judging the value of public relations activity. AVE had risen from fifth place to third in the five years since the previous study."[19]

However, PR practitioners are now being forced to improve. Various PR awards have banned the entry of work that is evaluated with AVEs. This is a good move. Like it or not, we live in a mathocracy. Business leaders require decent data which proves that expenditure is worthwhile. Weiner says that "audits" of the executives who fund PR activities find that what executives want is not coverage. Instead, they want to see results – easily measurable – such as how effective expenditure on PR has been at (a) raising awareness and (b) delivering key messages to the target audience.

Although measurement costs money, it does not have to be outrageously expensive. Lowish-cost tools for PR measurement include opinion polls of awareness and favourability towards the brand (taken before and after a campaign), microsites for particular PR campaigns and "How did you hear of us?" questioning

---

[19] Prof Tom Watson, "Advertising Value Equivalence – PR's orphan metric", http://eprints.bournemouth.ac.uk/20492/5/Tom%2520Watson%2520 -%2520Advertising%2520Value%2520Equivalence%2520%2528MS%2529%25 20R3.docx.pdf (accessed February 28, 2013).

when people buy. There is a lot of good material on designing measurement plans in a book by Tom Watson and Paul Noble, called *Evaluating Public Relations*, and the Public Relations Consultants Association runs a useful workshop training people how to use each type of measurement.

There are now several good books on the subject and the so-called "Barcelona Principles", set in 2010, have spurred on many at the elite end of the industry. Some of the biggest agencies and companies – such as AT&T and Procter & Gamble – have been able to deduce the return on investment that their PR campaigns produce. They've done this with marketing mix modelling, a useful tool for mid-sized and large companies.

The results from such modelling can be astounding. As Mark Weiner reports, the Miller Brewing Company, part of SABMiller, found that every additional $1 spent on TV advertising brought a return of $1.06, while PR delivered $8. (The company has subsequently changed its advertising agency.) Ranjit Choudhary, the marketing mix modelling specialist for Miller, said in 2003: "We found that PR was much more efficient than other promotions for the brand."[20]

What I find most useful about decent measurement is that it can redirect what PR practitioners work on. This is because companies often guess about the sort of coverage that benefits them most. If they rely on this guesswork, without testing it, the PR activities may fail to deliver the best results.

---

[20] Mark Weiner, "PR and Meaningful Business Outcome", http://www.prime -research.com/attachments/3301_Prove%20PR%20Value.Improve%20PR%20 Performance.pdf (accessed February 23, 2013).

What is vital, whatever size of business you are, is to compare your media coverage with that of your competitors, and with your results in the previous year. It will encourage you to push ahead, and be a source of ideas.

So what is the best way of tracking your press coverage? These days PR practitioners tend to receive scanned press cuttings in their email inbox, provided by a media monitoring service. The most highly regarded provider in the UK is Precise, which will also provide recordings of radio and television mentions. There are similar suppliers around the world. For online cuttings, services such as Google News Alerts, which is free, will email you, more or less, whenever your company name, or a preferred phrase, is written on the web.

What to avoid

In the next chapter, we will start to look at how to create a compelling PR campaign. But let's first debunk some myths.

Critics of public relations describe its practitioners as "spin doctors" and believe that its role is pernicious. Spin is not good public relations. It is counterproductive idiocy. The term arose during the late 1990s, when political figures in the UK and America ditched authenticity and just put out what they thought was politically palatable. The result? Lots of news stories appeared discussing how the government was issuing fake data and announcing expenditure in a misleading way. The spin doctors themselves become the story, damaging the reputation of their masters.

Andrew Marr, a BBC news show host and former Editor of *The Independent*, explained the problem:[21]

> Things got so bad that even when Blair [as British Prime Minister] was saying something obvious, he was disbelieved.
>
> "Well, the spin is that . . ." began a thousand reports. Media cynicism curdled further. The spinning became angrier still.

Ivy Lee, the inventor of the press release and a pioneer in crisis communications, had a better approach. He traded under the slogan "Accuracy, Authenticity, and Interest". These three terms were not a sign of uncommercial naivety. The man was extremely well paid and was retained by the Rockefellers and the steel magnate Charles M. Schwab. Instead, his ethical position ensured that his messages were convincing.

In the 1930s, A. H. Wiggin, Chairman of the Chase National Bank, ordered Lee to get a newspaper to kill a story. "I won't do anything of the sort," Lee replied. His advice, instead, was to issue a statement so that their side of the story would be aired.

Those three terms in Lee's slogan, "Accuracy, Authenticity, and Interest", remain today at the core of good public relations. Lee's "Declaration of Principles", issued to newspapers in 1906, are still – more than a century later – some of the best words ever written on the duty of public relations practitioners. He declared:

> This is not a secret press bureau. All our work is done in the open. We aim to supply news. This is not an advertising agency; if you think any of our matter ought properly to go to your business [advertising] office, do not use it. Our matter is accurate. Further details on any subject treated will be supplied promptly, and any

---

[21] Andrew Marr, BBC News, http://news.bbc.co.uk/1/hi/uk_politics/6638231 .stm (accessed February 23, 2013).

editor will be assisted most cheerfully in verifying directly any statement of fact. Upon inquiry, full information will be given to any editor concerning those on whose behalf an article is sent out. In brief, our plan is, frankly and openly, on behalf of business concerns and public institutions, to supply to the press and public of the United States prompt and accurate information concerning subjects which it is of value and interest to the public to know about. Corporations and public institutions give out much information in which the news point is lost to view. Nevertheless, it is quite as important to the public to have this news as it is to the establishments themselves to give it currency. I send out only matter every detail of which I am willing to assist any editor in verifying for himself. I am always at your service for the purpose of enabling you to obtain more complete information concerning any of the subjects brought forward in my copy.

Fraser Seitel, a heavyweight of the American PR industry, who, like Lee before him, has represented the Rockefeller family, says: "Ivy Lee really, really preached that the public has to be informed, and if your policies are not good and not in the public interest, you have to change the policy. And I think that this is what a lot of people don't recognise about the practice of public relations, if you believe it as I do, that it starts with policy, it starts with performance, it starts with action . . . You can't pour perfume on a skunk."[22]

When PR won't work

In the mid-1990s, I was a columnist for IDG, the world's largest publisher of IT magazines. When writing a particular comparative

---

[22] http://www.alexsingleton.com/real-crisis-communications-never-defends
-the-indefensible/ (accessed February 23, 2013).

review, I realised that one of the products was awful. It came from a micro-business and I thought that few people, realistically, were likely to ever buy it. While I wrote the odd negative review, on this occasion I did the company a favour and excluded mentioning their product in my article.

I later heard that the firm's proprietor had been moaning to a journalist on another magazine that he'd gone to great trouble, personally driving across London to put it through my letterbox – and I never bothered to mention it!

Here's the rub: PR only works properly if your product is good. Journalists aren't stupid – well, not for the most part – and they can smell if your product is second-rate. What determines if a product is good? Well, in the 1940s, Rosser Reeves, the American advertising guru, invented the concept of a "unique selling proposition". In his 1961 book *Reality in Advertising*, Reeves says that "the proposition must be one that the competition either cannot, or does not, offer".

Just as the "unique selling proposition" is vital for selling to consumers through advertising, it is vital when pitching to journalists. If you're manufacturing camera bags (to go back to my example) that fall to bits and have no obvious benefits, the media are going to be less keen on promoting you.

The miracle cure

Lots of companies will try to sell you the miracle cure to media relations. If only you throw money at a newswire service, or a social media planning tool or a special media database of over a million journalists, something great is supposed to happen.

Some of these can be of help, but only if you are doing all the other things right. In fact, many of the really useful tools are free, or not specifically aimed at media relations. I will recommend some in this book. But I find that just three tools are the ones I definitely need to get coverage: email, a telephone and a copy of the publication. All the others are optional.

One miracle cure that must, in all circumstances, be avoided is the so-called professional press release writer – someone who, for a very cheap price, will write you a release. People who use these services believe erroneously that the value in public relations is in the press release. This is mistaken. For a start, the value that a so-called press release writer will give you is likely to be small. One, I notice, is offering a "media friendly press release in two hours" that will "get you coverage in all the right places".

But the vendor then goes on to say: "I would need a brief outline of what you want to achieve, the what, when, where, why and of [sic] the story. As well as a few short quotes and a high res image. I would also need your website information and contact details of your public relations person."

Here, the customer is still doing almost all of the work – and the difficult part too. No wonder the seller wants just £15 for the service. Others are as cheap as £9.

Now it is certainly true that most press releases are badly written, poorly structured and fail to sell the story properly. But none of the people I've seen advertising this sort of service seem to reveal much about themselves or convincingly explain why they would produce something better than if you wrote it yourself.

Anyway, these sorts of services are beside the point, because the real problem businesses have is that the ideas *behind* their press releases are bad. A dirt cheap copywriter isn't going to solve that for you. What will are good, creative ideas, which we will be discussing in the next chapter.

Chapter 2

How to Develop a Story Idea that Is Newsworthy

At the heart of all good media relations is creativity. But how do you become creative? Well, not by waving a magic wand. Creativity requires *knowledge*, which provides a breeding ground for ideas. PR practitioners need to know intimately the products they are promoting. They need to read or watch closely the media outlets in which their clients want coverage. They need a strong general knowledge. And it helps if they study the great masters of public relations – such as Ivy Lee, Edward Bernays and Howard Gossage.

Why is knowledge so important? Well, according to James Webb Young (1886–1973), an advertising executive who wrote *A Technique For Producing Ideas*: "An idea is nothing more or less than a new combination of old elements".

And where do these elements come from? Well, Steve Harrison, the former worldwide creative director of ad agency Wunderman, wrote a book on creativity[23] in which he suggested the answer:

---

[23] Steve Harrison, *How to do Better Creative Work* (Pearson Education: Harlow, 2009), p. 6.

Be curious about the world around you. Read a different newspaper, drink in different bars, visit a new website a day, listen to a different radio station, eat at a different type of cafe or restaurant and book somewhere totally different next time you're planning your holidays . . . and find out what makes people "tick".

The trap that modern PR practitioners can fall into is homophily, the tendency of individuals to flock together with similar people. Following people who are like us on social networks and reading the same online articles risks limiting creativity because we don't experience radically different ideas. "We're getting narrower and narrower and more and more tribal," says Chris Graves, the global CEO of Ogilvy PR. "And so we're like an echo chamber of what we believe."[24]

That's why it can be advantageous to read print editions of publications, which encourage you – much more than online – to notice and read things that would not be your first choice of topic. And it makes radio talk shows a useful resource. Do you get woken up by a radio alarm clock? It is, in my view, a useful bit of kit.

The three types of news story

In this chapter, I predominately focus on news stories – of which there are three types. The first is the "sackable offence" – someone will be sacked if the story isn't covered. UK declares war on France. The US President announces tax cuts. New Apple iPhone launched. You won't have any difficulty in gaining coverage for these sort of rare stories.

---

[24] http://www.youtube.com/watch?v=-EdjNV8aHUw (accessed March 12, 2013).

Then there's the type represented by 90 per cent of press releases sent to newspapers. They are the stories that are so bad that no self-respecting newspaper would ever publish them. They exist because the senders don't know what they are doing or, more likely, because they are too scared to tell their clients that no will care. They belong to the all-too-common world of untrained junior practitioners, who never read the media and don't know what they want.

And then there's third type. The "maybe, maybe not" story idea. These are what good PR professionals spend most of their time on. These are stories where there is no guarantee of coverage, but with a good pitch and a bit of luck, you'll find your company or cause covered in print.

It's creating this third type of story that we're going to look at now.

The perspective of the journalist

If you have invented the cure for bone cancer, then your business is inherently interesting. Most businesses are not, at least not most of the time. It requires skill and creativity to turn what your company is doing into something newsworthy. Those who send out press releases announcing the minutiae of a business's dealings – especially if it is a small business – will just irritate journalists. In fact, for something to be genuinely newsworthy, it has to be out of the ordinary.

Journalists are frequently frustrated by the failure of PR people to understand what interests their readers. One technology PR firm – of some size, but not a member of the Public Relations

Consultants Association – routinely spams press releases to the national press saying that companies should invest more in "CRM systems".

This is wrong on at least two levels. Firstly, the vast majority of people have not the faintest idea what a "CRM system" is – and, what's more, probably don't want to know. It is, in fact, a database that companies use to track their customers' details. It stands for Customer Relationship Management system and records how much clients have been billed and the details of phone calls they have made to the company. So it's an important part of modern business, but – let's face it – normally boring to the general public.

Secondly, there is no "news hook" in simply saying that businesses should spend more on this software. By news hook, I mean such press releases do not connect with any existing theme in the news. The PR representatives might be able to gain some interest for their client's agenda when a major company has failed its customers through a faulty IT system, with a press release that reveals widespread underinvestment. A news hook is not necessary when a story is sufficiently important or interesting to force itself into the news regardless. But when pitching something specialist – like a CRM system – to mass-market, consumer titles, it is pretty essential.

So how does a news hook work? Well, let's say you sell something – gym membership – that helps cure obesity. You produce some new research which shows that people who go to the gym twice a week take half as many sick days as those who aren't members. That's pretty interesting. It would be most effective just after a major public figure has lashed out against the rising obesity epidemic. The public figure's speech would be the news hook. But obesity is also (how shall I say?) an issue of our age, and therefore interesting most of the time. In this case, you probably don't need a specific news hook. But a news hook always increases the probably of coverage, and normally increases the amount of space a publication will allocate to it.

Like the technology PR firm's spam, I came across a similar case of PR idiocy being committed by a bank. Its PR agency rang personal finance journalists on national papers in the UK every fortnight to read them the bank's interest rates. It got so annoying that one tabloid journalist took to exclaiming a profanity, before slamming down the handset.

These press releases or phone calls were being made so that the perpetrators could tick boxes to say that they had done the tasks allocated to them. In such examples, the PR practitioners deployed no creativity. So, in this chapter, we'll look at how creativity can be at the centre of your PR.

Below are several techniques to achieve good creative ideas. They are all optional, except the first, which should be incorporated into every PR campaign you do.

Luke Skywalker vs. Darth Vader

If you take any decent movie – in fact, any movie – you'll notice that there is conflict. In Star Wars, the conflict is between the rebels, such as Luke Skywalker, and the Empire, most notably represented by Darth Vader. The tension between the two sides is what makes it interesting.

Even in more subtle movies, there is tension. In *The Cider House Rules*, the protagonist, Homer Wells, is torn in a whole variety of ways, including between following the path set for him by his surrogate father, and pursuing experiences elsewhere. There isn't a villain incarnate, but the scriptwriters have included conflict, because otherwise we wouldn't watch the film.

That same tension is a requirement for media relations. For example, when Apple launches a new version of its operating system, the media invariably writes about how it compares with Microsoft Windows. This is also why politics gets so much coverage – journalists know that the readers love hearing about the battles between the main parties.

That is not to say that you should declare war on competitors in your press releases, although occasionally it is the right strategy (we'll discuss the "grenade" strategy later in this chapter). Instead, you can just describe your product as "the fastest on the market". The media, where relevant, will make explicit comparisons themselves. And the enemy – the Darth Vader – of the story may not be another company, but a worse alternative. For example, a company that rescues a High Street by buying a bankrupt shop (which it will turn around) is not fighting against another company, but a boarded-up street.

A good example of using conflict effectively is this press release from Kellogg's:[25]

---

[25] Kellogg's News Release, http://pressoffice.kelloggs.co.uk/index.php?s=20295 &item=122395 (accessed March 12, 2013).

Millions of British women could literally be talking themselves fat

Women should cut out the negative "fat talk" if they want to successfully lose weight, a new report has revealed.

As millions of British women get ready to embark on a New Year diet, new research . . . has revealed they could be setting up for failure by describing themselves as "fat", "heavy" or "chubby".

Eight in ten women said they believed a positive attitude was the key to losing weight even though over half of women said when starting a diet they are more likely to be self critical and use words such as "fat".

Here, the conflict is between obesity and a perfect weight. It is a surprising – and therefore interesting – press release. Who would have thought that *talking* about weight would make you fat?

Normally, you should be explicit in any press release about where the tension lies – just as the Kellogg's press release is. But sometimes, it will be sufficiently obvious that it is not necessary. Where a company submits its products for review, there is an implicit notion that they are in some way better than others. (If they weren't better, in any way, it would be stupid to try to get the media to look at them.)

For example, readers of *What Hi-Fi* are interested in whether a Marantz amplifier is better than a Cambridge Audio one. That is the conflict. In *Gramophone*, the classical music magazine, readers want to know if Stephen Hough's performance of Rachmaninov's Piano Concerto no 2 is better than Vladimir Ashkenazy's. The PR approaches that generate comparative reviews like these are unlikely to mention any rivals. But without there being any conflict or tension, explicit or implicit, a press release is unlikely to be very successful.

Opinion polls

News organisations love the results of opinion polls. They give authority to your story: merely asserting that the public believes something is nowhere near as convincing as showing that the public believes something with figures.

The mistake companies make is to cheapskate on the gathering of data. They perhaps use a survey of visitors to their website. The results lack credibility and newspapers won't touch them. To be taken seriously, you have to use a major polling agency such as YouGov, ComRes, Survation or Gallup. This costs money – although most polling agencies will help you do it inexpensively with a so-called Omnibus poll, which asks your questions along with those of their other clients.

Some thought needs to go into how the poll is set up. To be newsworthy, the poll results should say something significant. Normally, a poll where half of the population believe one thing and half don't isn't stark enough to justify coverage. An exception is election polling, where a difference of a few per cent can determine who takes office. But, in general, an ideal poll result shows a sizeable gap between one view and the other.

I noticed a poll done by Socked.co.uk, which had the start of something newsworthy, but did not quite nail it. Here's the beginning of the press release:[26]

Holy Sock! Most men's socks are over three years old

A survey by Socked.co.uk finds that nine out of ten women are turned off by the state of their partner's socks. The figures show that a huge majority of men are wearing socks that are more than three years old, will rarely – if ever – go shopping to replace them.

Worse, three-quarters of men admit to wearing odd socks when their tired old footwear has let them down, and have failed to act when others have commented on their appearance.

Nowhere in the press release did it say which polling agency conducted the poll or how large the sample size was. These are two essential items, because they are vital for convincing a journalist that a poll is credible. In general, a poll of 1,000 people is considered statistically reliable.

The most interesting result, that "nine out of ten women are turned off by the state of their partner's socks", is actually too

---

[26] Socked Press Room, http://news.cision.com/socked-co-uk/r/holy-sock–most -men-s-socks-are-over-three-years-ol,c9323432 (accessed March 12, 2013).

vague. "Turned off" could mean they engage in less sexual intercourse or are just disappointed in a non-sexual way. Later in the press release, the company claims that this is "The killer blow for men's libido". But the question asked doesn't actually establish that convincingly. A good polling agency would have helped them clarify the questions they were asking.

Data and research

In a similar vein to opinion polls, data and research from other sources is highly prized by media outlets. Routinely, newspapers print stories with headlines that end "research says" or "scientists say". In the next chapter we will look at how one company took freely available figures from government statistics, ran a simple spreadsheet calculation and got substantial coverage across the UK.

Reframing how we view the world

Travelodge ran a PR campaign suggesting that it is more economical to put guests up in a Travelodge than to have an extra bedroom that's only used once or twice a year.[27] The campaign attempted to reframe how consumers view the expenditure. Whereas normally using a hotel would be viewed as a loss (wastes money), Travelodge presented it as a gain (saves substantially on the mortgage). The press release began:

---

[27] http://www.telegraph.co.uk/finance/2952812/Business-profile-Christmas -room-for-all-at-Grants-inn.html (accessed March 12, 2013).

> Over 15 million Brits own homes with more bedrooms than they need, a situation that's costing homeowners more than £20,000 each over the life of their mortgage.
>
> Almost half of all British homeowners (45%) cite being able to accommodate visiting friends and family as the main reason for buying an over-sized property.
>
> However, according to a new study from Travelodge, almost a fifth of British homeowners have never had relatives or friends stay overnight and just two per cent say it happens once a week.
>
> On average, Brits put up friends just six times a year, and relatives even more infrequently at five times. Only using a room a few times each year is an expensive habit, costing the homeowner approximately £155 each visit.

This got Travelodge a good deal of coverage. Importantly, the press release went on to name the polling agency, 72Point, and explain that certain figures were sourced from other reputable sources, such as the Office for National Statistics.

Gamification

Have you ever noticed that computer games are addictive? I didn't play for about 15 years, and then got an Xbox. In the intervening years, the games have become like movies, with scripts as complex and picture quality that's almost as good. I find myself playing for what seems like 20 minutes – but is, in fact, two hours.

The same thing happens in sport: people happily spend 90 minutes glued to a televised soccer match. This is, let's face it, just 22 people kicking a ball about – but turned into a game, it entertains millions.

So is there anything we can learn from the compelling nature of computer games and sport? Such games contain problem-solving, escapism, competition, a sense of achievement and visible rewards, whether in goals, points, a virtual currency or achievement levels. The science of gamification tries to apply these to other fields – in our case, public relations.

Jesse Schell, Professor of Entertainment Technology at Carnegie Mellon University, defines gamification as "a problem solving situation which you enter into willingly . . . a symptom of something that is happening in the nature of design, which is that we're moving from a model where we design things to be efficient and effective, to where we design things so that we like them".[28]

In 1966, *Scientific American* wanted to sell more advertising to airlines. Its readers flew a lot, but it had failed to convey this to their airlines. The "efficient" technique, to use Professor Schell's terminology, would have been to issue a press release saying that advertisers should spend their money with the magazine. No one

---

[28] http://www.edge-online.com/features/dice-2011-schell-reynolds-debate -gamification/ (accessed March 12, 2013).

would have covered it. Or they could have placed some advertisements saying that their readers fly a lot. That would have
been somewhat effective.

Instead, the company turned to Howard Gossage, a master of
advertising and public relations, who created a campaign based
on gamification. The magazine announced the 1st International
Paper Airplane Competition, promoted with a single advertisement, a press conference and huge newspaper coverage. It generated nearly 12,000 entries, including 5,000 from children. A book
of the best entries, *The Great International Paper Airplane Book*, was
a best-seller. The airlines fell in love with the magazine.

The Royal Society of Chemistry in London did something
similar in 2008, when it challenged the public to come up with a
solution to the cliffhanger in the movie *The Italian Job*. How, they
asked, could Charlie Croker, the film's protagonist, and his team,
extract the gold within 30 minutes, without using a helicopter –
and how could it be proved mathematically? This engaged the
readers of *The Daily Telegraph*'s letters page over many days,
while increasing awareness of the practical uses of science. The
paper ran a substantial story under the headline "Cliffhanger
climax to *The Italian Job* solved after 40-year wait."[29]

Although gamification is too rarely used today, Edward
Bernays – a founding father of public relations – was using the
technique in the first half of the 20th century. For Procter &
Gamble, he ran the National Soap Sculpture Competition in

---

[29] http://www.telegraph.co.uk/science/science-news/4315767/Cliffhanger
-climax-to-The-Italian-Job-solved-after-40-year-wait.html (accessed March 12,
2013).

White Soap, which convinced children to drop their hostility to soap and start using P&G's Ivory brand. By the fourth time the contest was run, 4,000 entries were submitted, and schools around the United States were involved.

The bandwagon

The term "bandwagon" originated in 19th-century American politics. A famous circus clown called Dan Rice helped Zachary Taylor win the 1848 presidential election. He invited the politician on to his bandwagon (literally "a wagon used for carrying a band in a parade or procession",[30] which was often elaborately decorated). This was a major success and other political campaigns started to use bandwagons in their campaigns. Subsequently, politicians would physically jump on to better-known politicians' bandwagons in order to gain some of their stardust.

Most publications will have issues or campaigns that they care deeply about. Jumping on these bandwagons is an easy way of securing coverage in them. The simple task of reading the publications relevant to your industry, in addition to general news sources, will reveal which issues excite them. For example, in 2011 the *London Evening Standard* launched a campaign called Get London Reading. It pointed out that 1,000 children in the UK's capital leave primary school (aged 11) unable to read properly.[31]

---

[30] Oxford Dictionaries, http://oxforddictionaries.com/definition/english/bandwagon?q=bandwagon (accessed February 24, 2013).

[31] "Success of our literacy campaign inspires imitators across" in the London Evening Standard, December 12, 2013, http://www.standard.co.uk/news/get-london-reading/success-of-our-literacy-campaign-inspires-imitators-across-the-uk-8411312.html (accessed February 24, 2012).

The paper set about fundraising for the literacy charity Beanstalk.

Specsavers, a franchised chain of opticians, promptly jumped in and raised a significant sum for the campaign.[32] It was a good fit, because glasses help people to read well, and the campaign is about reading. The newspaper reported that the opticians had raised £32,000, "by completing a year of gruelling physical challenges", including mountain climbing and a marathon cycling race. The money would pay for 64 reading mentors to go into primary schools. It was excellent publicity for the company.

The grenade

This is not a technique that I would advise everyone to use. It depends very much on your position in the marketplace and on what sort of product you are selling. It is never, I would say, appropriate for a luxury goods company, which should rise above using it. But it has been used effectively by challenger brands, who use it to grab some of the limelight from the market leader.

What it involves is using a press release, and perhaps an associated stunt, that acts a bit like throwing a grenade at the rest of the industry. Steve Ballmer, the Chief Executive Officer of Microsoft, gained considerable press coverage when he criticised his

---

[32] "Specsavers staff go to great lengths to raise £32,000 for young readers" in the London Evening Standard, November 16, 2012, http://www.standard.co.uk/news/get-london-reading/specsavers-staff-go-to-great-lengths-to-raise-32000-for-young-readers-8322794.html (accessed February 24, 2012).

two rivals in the smartphone industry, who were both outselling his company. He was widely quoted saying[33]:

> The ecosystem of the Android is a little bit wild, that is from an app compatibility perspective and our world perspective maybe in a way that's not always in the consumer's best interests. Conversely the Apple ecosystem looks highly controlled, and, by the way, quite high priced.

His comments were not vicious, but they contradicted the sometimes held view that a company should never criticise a competitor. Steve Jobs, co-founder of Apple, was not adverse to this technique, accusing a rival, Adobe, of being "lazy"[34] and saying that Adobe's Flash product "is a spaghetti-ball piece of technology that has lousy performance and really bad security problems". Ouch. Those quotes secured a lot of coverage.

But the grenade is a risky approach because it is quite possible that, in return, a victim will pull out the pin in one of their own grenades and lob criticism in your direction. You have to be thick skinned to use the technique and confident that there is nothing about your company that would humiliate you were a competitor to spend a couple of hours looking into your business.

It can sometimes be deployed not as a direct hit, but under the cover of trying to be helpful. When British Airways staff went on

---

[33] The Telegraph, "Microsoft CEO Steve Ballmer attacks Android and Apple", http://www.telegraph.co.uk/technology/microsoft/9680725/Microsoft-CEO -Steve-Ballmer-attacks-Android-and-Apple.html (accessed February 23, 2013).
[34] ZDNet, "Steve Jobs calls Adobe 'lazy', says Google can't 'kill the iPhone' ", http://www.zdnet.com/blog/gadgetreviews/steve-jobs-calls-adobe-lazy-says -google-cant-kill-the-iphone/11925 (accessed February 23, 2013).

strike, Michael O'Leary, the head of rival Ryanair, gave some advice to BA via the press. "The unions need to be taken on", he said. "BA is massively over-staffed and has got to get its costs down." But he added that "I think, like most flag carriers do, they'll wimp out at the eleventh hour. The problem for [BA chief executive] Willie Walsh is that the board of BA has no spine, no balls and no vision." The result? Press coverage under the headline "British Airways lacks the spine to fight union, says Ryanair".[35]

The grenade can also tarnish an entire industry if it is used too frequently. Witness how much everyone hates politicians – they lob metaphorical grenades at each other every day. It can also damage relationships with companies you want to work with. When cable operator Virgin Media was in dispute with Sky, which produces several popular channels, it replaced Sky News with an on-screen message saying "Sky Snooze try BBC". Richard Branson, the founder of Virgin, ordered the removal of the message. He told *The Guardian*: "I have asked them to take it down. We do not mean any disrespect to Sky News. I think it is a very good news channel."[36]

Days and weeks

One technique that some PR campaigns use is to create a special day, week or even fortnight of the year to mark an issue. There

---

[35] Alistair Osborne, *The Telegraph*, February 24, 2010, http://www.telegraph.co.uk/finance/newsbysector/transport/7301234/British-Airways-lacks-the-spine-to-fight-union-says-Ryanair.html (accessed February 24, 2013).

[36] "Branson puts stop to 'Sky Snooze' joke", *The Guardian*, http://www.guardian.co.uk/media/2007/mar/02/bskyb.broadcasting1 (accessed February 24, 2013).

is Red Nose Day in the UK, which raises money for the charity Comic Relief. Hundreds of thousands of children buy plastic red noses – or, at least, their parents buy them – and many engage in charity-themed events at school. In the evening, the BBC broadcasts a fundraising programme containing performances from well-known comedians.

In the United States, National History Day involves more than 500,000 school students, who enter an academic competition by producing a paper, documentary or exhibit. The day is sponsored by, among others, The History Channel, and has gained coverage everywhere from *The New York Times* to Fox News.

If a "day" or "week" is commercial, rather than in aid of charity, it is vital that it is fun. Chocolate Week is an example of a week working well, with coverage across national newspapers and broadcasters. It helps that it is an industry-wide event, rather than promoting just one supplier.

So, should you use the technique of creating a "day" or "week" to mark some cause, in the aim of gaining publicity? Rarely, in my view, because most of the people who try to do this fail. I have a friend who graduated with an excellent history degree during the recession at the beginning of the 1990s. He was unable to get a job, so set himself up as a self-employed grave-digger. Seeing the funny side of having a history BA, but doing the most menial of tasks, he sent a press release to major national newspapers. Soon he was being interviewed by a feature writer and having his photograph taken by a press photographer. Seeing that it gained him publicity, he later announced National Grave-digging Day. It didn't work. None of the press were interested. Why was this?

Well, news organisations endlessly receive press releases promoting some day or other, and the media is suspicious about them. Journalists think that most of them do not actually involve many participants. This public involvement is what makes a day or week newsworthy. Remember, newspapers want to publish things that their readers find interesting, and so PR exercises such as "Green Office Week", promoted by an office stationary company, are largely ignored.

A journalist never wants to be accused of writing an advertisement. She is constrained by reputation, both the reputation with colleagues and also with the readers. She may personally like the PR practitioner, but she may be reluctant to write about a "day" which feels like an advert for a company. Indeed, most of the days which are promoted are created very much with the needs of the vendor in mind, not the journalist or reader.

My grave-digging friend, by the way, went on to run a successful PR agency, which gets clients into publications throughout the year. In fact, the best PR practitioners pitched plenty of stories that didn't work well when they were starting out. A difference between good PR practitioners and bad ones is that the former analyse what went wrong and learn from the mistakes, while the bad ones simply blame the media.

Scarcity

From economics, we know that scarcity increases something's value. Services such as Pinterest and Gmail gained considerable coverage when they were not generally available. They were launched with closed beta tests, and you had to persuade an existing user to invite you to join. Articles such as "How to Get a Pinterest Invite" appeared on blogs and were widely tweeted. Journalists loved writing about these services because they were part of the small number of people who could actually see the products. Therefore, there were lots of readers keen to read up on the functionality offered.

Diary stories

Some specialist titles and many newspapers have what are called "diary columns", which cover the comings and goings of notable people. They rose to prominence after the *Daily Mail* started publishing such a column under the pseudonym William Hickey in 1928. Some cover high society, some cover politics, and trade titles tend to cover figures in the industry. These articles normally contain a selection of short stories – maybe four or five – in the same column.

If a trade title covering your sector has a diary column, it is a good place to get coverage. A diary column might contain gossipy stories about the sector along with entertaining photographs of major industry characters. Such columns are worth studying, before contacting with stories that are in a similar vein. I happen to know that at least one major PR agency gave its staff the task of getting into PRWeek's now-defunct diary column as one of its staff's "Key Performance Indicators", although this struck me as a little keen.

The best way to approach diary columns is not to sit round a table struggling to come up with an idea to submit. Instead, I find it more effective simply to read them and when – by chance – something funny occurs, then think about emailing the publication.

Product reviews

Moving on from news, often the most useful form of coverage is the product review. These don't require you to apply a lot of imagination, but you would be amazed at how many requests for a review are inappropriate. It is vital that a PR practitioner does the legwork to find where, if anywhere, in the publication the review would naturally fit. Some publications don't review products, or have criteria that will be apparent to regular readers, which might not fit what you are selling.

It is often worth pitching directly to someone who has reviewed similar products, especially if they are a freelancer and are keen themselves to secure more work. In the pre-internet days, it was difficult to track down freelancers. Nowadays, they probably have a website, or a presence on Twitter or LinkedIn.

The best PR practitioners never supply a product to a reviewer on its own. They include a short reviewer's guide, containing important information about its advantages and features. This will help a journalist understand the product properly and not overlook its main benefits, especially if bashing out the review quickly. You may find that the journalist agrees that many of the points you highlight in your guide are indeed important, and find that he or she refers to them in the review.

It helps to record the contact details of reviewers, especially if they are freelance. This will save a huge amount of time when you next want a product to be reviewed, because you will have a ready distribution list of people who find your products worthy of coverage. Indeed, it will stop endless frustrating conversations along the lines of: "Who's that reviewer in Cleveland who wrote that really positive review last time? I wish we had her number."

The specific challenge of business-to-business stories

People often get unstuck when trying to get coverage for companies that sell to other companies, rather than to individuals. They find that newspapers and consumer titles fail to cover them. There are two ways to resolve this.

The first is to say that newspapers and consumer titles are aimed at the general public. While it may be good for the ego to get coverage in them, the actual readership is likely to be less interested in buying than the readership of a trade title. Seasoned PR practitioners all have tales of senior management or clients who want glamorous coverage that serves no commercial purpose, and is essentially only placed for reasons of vanity. From a purely rational point of view, it is better to concentrate on the trade press.

The second is to say that business-to-business PR campaigns need to change the angle of their press releases, and start talking about their products from the perspective of the ultimate consumer. After all, not every potential business customer will read a trade title, and in many cases there is no trade title covering the potential customer base. Let me give the example of CardSave, a provider of credit card terminals to small businesses. They are, therefore, a business-to-business vendor, but how many small businesses subscribe to *Credit Card Terminal Weekly* (hint: it doesn't exist)?

The company gained huge coverage in the *Daily Mail* by being interesting to consumers. The *Mail*'s story appeared under the headline "Cash will all but die out by 2032, says expert, as small businesses accepting card payments double in five years".[37] The article quoted the head of CardSave extensively, and was newsworthy on the back of a survey that the company commissioned. "The survey", the paper reported, "found that 57 per cent of people believe that cash will become extinct in the future – 50 per cent predict that it will happen by 2035 and 36 per cent by 2025".

A similar example occurred when a manufacturer of scientific weighing scales, Kern & Sohn, wanted to raise its sales, by standing out in a marketplace where brand recognition is poor. They ran an experiment, with the aid of the scientific public. It turns out that the world is not completely spherical, which means that objects, on ordinary scales, weigh a slightly different amount depending upon where they are located on the planet.

The firm launched a microsite – that is, a small cluster of pages separate from its main website – where people could volunteer to borrow a pair of the scales and a garden gnome. A gnome's arrival on the South Pole grabbed substantial media coverage. The experiment was covered on major channels from the BBC to Canada's CBC News and Australia's ABC, and in publications from *National Geographic* to *The Times*. By the end of the first week of the campaign 1,445 sales leads had been generated. Thousands of people volunteered to participate in the weighing and the media coverage eventually reached an estimated audience of more than 350 million people in 152 countries.

---

[37] Lee Boyce, "Cash will all but die out by 2032, says expert", *Daily Mail*, April 24, 2013, http://www.dailymail.co.uk/money/saving/article-2133899/Cash -die-2032-says-expert-small-businesses-accepting-card-payments-double-years .html (accessed February 26, 2013).

Chapter 3

How to Build and Maintain an Effective List of Journalists

W hat is the biggest mistake people make when pitching to the press? It is to think that having a rented database of journalists means that they do not need to personally concern themselves with learning about any individual writers. There are huge databases with 1.5 million media contacts worldwide, containing newspaper reporters, television and radio editors and even bloggers. They sound like a fantastic shortcut. Just like get-rich-quick schemes, which promise financial success without doing much work, these seem to tell you which journalists to contact without needing to read and research the publications.

But you might as well just send your press release to everyone in the phone book.

As a result of the lazy use of these databases by bad PR people, journalists are endlessly harassed by press releases that they have no interest in. A PR practitioner pays somewhere between £900 and £4,500 a year for one of these media databases. Because they have spent so much money on it, they feel that they need to get value for money out of it, so they export 500 journalists and send their press release to all of them.

It has been estimated that 1.7 billion irrelevant press release emails were sent in 2009 alone.[38]

This spamming has got so bad that British trade bodies and unions including the Public Relations Consultants Association, the Chartered Institute of Public Relations and the National Union of Journalists introduced a "Media Spamming Charter", in which they wrote: "Practitioners should invest time in researching the editorial scope and interests of a journalist/blogger before approaching them, to ensure their area of responsibility is relevant to the communications plan."

It irritates journalists to receive mass-distributed press releases because it is obvious to them that they are being spammed: these press releases just aren't relevant to most of their recipients.

Charles Arthur, the Technology Editor of *The Guardian* (i.e. a computing and consumer technology journalist), wrote on his blog about the irrelevant press releases he receives, including from people who spam him assuming that his job as a tech journalist makes him interested in heavy plant machinery:[39]

> This is always done with no regard or interest or even checking as to whether the journalist is interested, or has ever written about this topic. That's because . . . it costs the PR nothing to send the email; the annoyed journalists' wasted time simply doesn't show up on the balance sheet.

---

[38] http://inconvenientprtruth.com/research/ (accessed March 3, 2013).

[39] http://www.charlesarthur.com/blog/index.php/2010/01/06/how-pr-fail -works-or-fails-to-work/.

According to Stuart Bruce, a founder of the English PR agency Wolfstar:[40]

> Every single media database I've tried . . . churns out lots of irrelevant targets and misses others no matter what you put in.
>
> The databases give the illusion of research, but in reality are a lazy way out . . .

An effective press release is unlikely to go to many people – and sometimes the pitch will be entirely bespoke for each journalist. Moreover, my experience of using most of the databases is they are inevitably out of date, because journalists move around more quickly than they are updated.

However, there is – at the time of writing – one media database that is actually good. I promise I'm not being paid to say this, but Precise Connect is a dramatic improvement on what has existed previously. It works well because every day around a million articles are added to the system, which stores them for 18 months. You can then search for everyone who has written about a subject in the past 18 months, regardless of what their job title is (and Precise has a global database of contacts, comprehensively covering major countries). Then, you can look at the articles they've written and see if you think a journalist is favourable to your position. You get the choice of either clicking to search for the web version of the article (this is free) or paying to view a PDF of the article from the print edition.

It is not a replacement for putting time into learning about journalists, but as a tool, it is actually useful.

---

[40] http://stuartbruce.biz/2010/02/an-inconvenient-pr-truth-experience-and -training-are-what-counts.html.

Pay-for press-release newswires

These services are mostly a waste of money, yet there is one advantage to them – which I'll come to towards the end. These sites promise to mail your press release to thousands of opted-in journalists, bloggers and "influencers", and promise to improve your company's search engine optimisation by putting an online press release on their website.

It all sounds a bit hocus pocus to me, and using them in the wrong way can cause more damage than good. They are, in the words of Heather Baker, Managing Director of TopLine Communications: "expertly designed to part fools from their money".[41]

Firstly, Google simply doesn't give much credibility to these online press releases. If you check the so-called Google PageRank of a press release on these press release websites, you'll see that they have a PageRank of zero. For search engine optimisation, you probably want sites with a PageRank of 5 or above linking to yours. But given that a release on a press release distribution site is likely to have no PageRank at all, any links to your site from those releases will fail to lend credibility to your site.

This is not just an opinion. The best-known authority in these matters is Matt Cutts, who is head of webspam at Google. He was asked about the strategy of using press releases to build links to a website. According to SearchEngineLand.com, he "clarified that the links in the press releases themselves don't count for PageRank value, but if a journalist reads the release and then

---

[41] http://b2bprblog.com/blog/2012/10/newswires-parting-fools-from-their -money-since-the-advent-of-the-internet.

writes about the site, any links in that news article will then count".[42]

Separately, on his blog, Cutts wrote: "a legit press release can get you written up by reporters, or editors/sites may subsequently choose to link to your site. But the actual content of the press release itself doesn't directly affect a site. For example, on [a press release about Avatar Financial on a distribution service's website] those hyperlinks don't help avatarfinancial.com."[43]

The question, therefore, is: how often do journalists actually pick up on what appears on online press release sites? For most journalists, the answer is surely never.

Some of these press release services say that they will get your article to appear on lots of websites. But what sort of website is likely to want to publish any old press release? Are they sites that relevant journalists or your customers are going to read? In 2011, Google took action against so-called "article directories" that were full of PR material placed there for the purpose of search engine optimisation. Google hates duplicate content, just as it hates webspam. As such, it is better to place your press releases on your own website.

Secondly, while I'm sure that these services do email many people who call themselves journalists, the vendors are not at all transparent about *which* journalists receive them. I, for one, have never come across a salaried journalist who subscribes to such

---

[42] http://searchengineland.com/lessons-learned-at-smx-west-googles
-farmerpanda-update-white-hat-cloaking-and-link-building-67838.
[43] http://www.mattcutts.com/blog/seo-article-in-newsweek/#comment-5925.

services. After all, why would they want their inbox bombarded with the stuff? It seems to be likely that the recipients are mostly freelance journalists – which these days typically means unemployed people. According to the New York news website Gawker. com: "A few writers (and many bloggers) ask for press pitches; readers can guess what that means about the quality of these outlets' material."[44]

What the pay-for newswires may achieve is one thing: they may get your story to appear on Google News. That might be worthwhile for you – and it has been for me. I put out a press release on one of those services. It was read by someone employed in a PR department in Paris and they paid for a first-class return Eurostar journey to attend an event. It did not, however, cause any journalists to get in touch.

In theory, using press release distribution services might be good if you are trying to piggy-back on a breaking news story and want to position yourself as a potential expert for television and radio stations. Journalists searching on Google News to find out what others are writing may see your press release. But this is only likely to work if producers are finding it very difficult to secure a guest.

There is another important consideration, which can make using these services backfire. If you're embargoing a story for a particular date, and send it out on one of these newswires, the moment it appears on Google News, the embargo is dead. You

---

[44] Nick Douglas, *Gawker*, http://valleywag.com/200494/dont-be-a-flack-tips -for-pr-workers-from-the-journalists-who-hate-them (accessed February 23, 2013).

won't be able to enforce it. (We will talk about the pros and cons of embargoing in Chapter 5.)

So, if pay-for newswires are of minimal use, why is it that films and dramas refer to "the wires", as though they are important? Well, a number of them are. It's just that the ones the media use are paid for by the media, not the PR practitioners. They are hand-crafted by teams of journalists and filter out all the worthless press releases and report on the genuinely newsworthy.

If your story is picked up by one of these, such as the Press Association or the Associated Press newswires, you are likely to get a lot of coverage. I cover how to interact with these agencies in Chapter 4.

How to build a list properly

The good news is that there are four cheaper and more effective ways of building a list of journalists.

The first – which I do religiously – is to add journalists I come across to a section of my Filofax. Every time I read a newspaper or magazine and come across a byline of someone I think I should contact in the future, I jot their name and publication down. This is a surprisingly effective technique, because actually reading a journalist's article(s) will do more to improve your pitches than anything else. Periodically, I sit with my Filofax and computer, research a journalist's back catalogue of articles and add her name to my computer. You can find out what software I currently prefer to use at www.alexsingleton.com/software.

The second, if the publication has a website, is to visit it online and use its search facility. If you represent a new brand of gin and tonic, and you want to pitch a story related to the drink, you could go on to *The Guardian*'s website and type in "gin and tonic". You can sort by date and find out who has written about the subject recently and decide which journalist or journalists at the paper would be most interested in your story.

If you don't recognise the journalist's name, the newspaper website might contain some biographical information, or a Google search might deliver this.

Using a news website's search facility will deliver much better results than most of the media databases, because it will be more comprehensive. If you are pitching a story about antiques, you are unlikely to find any journalist with the title "antiques correspondent" in a media database. But if you search for "antiques" on a newspaper website, you are likely to find more relevant general news reporters or features writers who have written about antiques previously. If you pitch to them directly, you might find that they are keen to write something.

The third way of building a list is to use an archive of publications, which are most notably provided by LexisNexis and Factiva. Their search facilities let you type in any subject and they will give you every article written about it in major publications. Importantly, they contain articles that have appeared in print publications but which never made it to the web.

The fourth way is to invite journalists who are visiting your website to join your press release distribution list. It is possible that there are journalists who are also your customers. They already love what you are doing, and would jump at the chance of writing about you. Therefore, you ought to have a "media centre" on your website and encourage the press to sign up. There is more on how to organise an online media centre in the next chapter.

How to build a relationship with the press

When I got my first column in 1994, in a newsstand computer magazine, I had no idea what I was doing. But it seemed like I needed to get some stories, so I wrote to all the relevant companies and invited them to send me information about what they were doing. Not all of them replied – those that failed to respond were PR idiots. Some of them wrote to me saying that they would add me to their press release distribution lists – they were amateurs.

Then some guy called Quentin got in touch. His company, Accountz, sold products by mail order and it was miniscule – just him and his wife. But he wrote me a personal two-page letter (this was before email was commonplace) explaining how he had a Big Idea to defeat the major players in his sector. Unlike some of the other companies, he had no PR agency – but he had a story. And during the 15 issues I wrote that column, I could always rely on him to take my calls and give me a good quote. When I upgraded to bigger-selling PC titles, including the market-leading *ComputerActive*, I kept on writing about his company. Today, his products are sold in PC World, Currys, AppleStores and Staples, and as I type this he has just made a successful exit from the company, passing it on to an investor.

What worked about that PR–journalist relationship is that Quentin – perhaps unwittingly – had good personal brand. He never tried to force a bad story on me and never wasted my time.

Marketing textbooks talk about the importance of a company brand, but anyone who's pitching to a journalist has a second brand to worry about: their personal brand. I get called by PR agencies and asked if I will help them pitch to the media a press release they've already written. I always refuse that sort of work, as I know they've rung me because the media isn't interested. It would be bad for my personal brand to ring journalists with bad stories, so I only pitch if I've been involved in the earlier creative process.

If you're dealing with the press regularly, they will get to recognise your name. Lots of PR people's emails never even make it to a journalist's inbox. That is either because they end up being spam filtered, or – as is increasingly common – because the journalist gets so fed up with the worthless material in them that he creates a filter to automatically divert a particular sender's messages to the bin.

Some clever journalists have discovered ways of automatically blocking all messages sent directly through media database services. Peter Kafka, Senior Editor at the Dow Jones-owned technology website AllThingsD.com, launched a Twitter attack on one of the most famous media databases, saying "Please stop using them. I'm setting up a filter to delete all their pitches."[45]

What you want is for the journalist to get a warm fuzzy feeling when you pop up in their inbox. How do you achieve that?

First, you need to be picky about what you send them. We will look at how to create a newsworthy story in the next chapter.

---

[45] Jeremy Bencken, "PR Spam is a Tools Problem", http://www.buzzstream.com/blog/vocus-pr-spam-kafka.html (accessed February 27, 2013).

Second, don't make every contact a request for coverage. For example, you ought to be following your target journalists on social media. Sometimes they'll ask their friends or followers for help. If you can assist, especially if it's not related to what you are selling, jump in and offer your advice.

While there are some journalists who are showered with praise and correspondence and offers of undying admiration, most get little feedback from what they do. They notice – and like it – if you share their content on social media, or write a blog highlighting the significance of what they have written. A word of caution: you need to be authentic, but showing that you are genuinely interested in what they are writing will do you well.

Third, get to meet the journalist. That doesn't necessarily mean a boozy lunch, which is much less common among journalists than it used to be. Most reporters find themselves tied to their desks at lunchtime, and pop out for a quick sandwich. As Professors Morris and Goldsworthy put it: "Keeping journalists in the office, tied to their computers, makes it easier to assess their productivity."[46] They refer to a study which suggests that British journalists have to write three times as much as they did 20 years ago. That's hardly surprising when you consider the average number of editorial pages in a selection of major British national newspapers ballooned from 26.4 in 1995 to 41 in 2006.[47] Meanwhile, internet publishing has provided significant opportunities for publishing extra content.

---

[46] Trevor Morris and Simon Goldsworthy, *PR Today* (London: Palgrave MacMillan, 2012), p. 32.

[47] "The Quality and Independence of British Journalism", http://www.cardiff.ac.uk/jomec/resources/QualityIndependenceofBritishJournalism.pdf (accessed March 1, 2013).

So journalists simply have less time to meet people. As such, there are lots of meetings that go on over breakfast these days, especially with financial journalists. Many one-to-ones happen quickly over coffee at newspaper offices. But you may find that a beer after work or a "chance" meeting at a trade show will work better, especially as the journalist then is unlikely to be worrying about deadlines.

You will also find that the more colourful journalists do speaking engagements and a bit of research on Google may reveal opportunities to meet them. I routinely go to major exhibitions and conferences in London where relevant journalists are likely to be present – perhaps on their magazine's stand – introduce myself and have a quick chat.

The purpose of meeting a journalist is not to harangue them into writing about you. It may be that you give them materials related to a future story. But it may be just to introduce yourself and let them know the sort of things you are working on and find out from them what they are really looking for.

Journalists, for the most part, don't want to have meetings with press officers, unless they are seen as having clout in their own right. A political journalist would normally be delighted to have a meeting with the Director of Communications at Number 10, but less so with a Junior Account Manager at a small PR agency. Generally, journalists want to meet the person in charge – e.g. the entrepreneur, the chief executive or the head of research. The job of a PR executive is to set up that sort of meeting, and perhaps sit in on it.

In the BBC comedy series *Absolute Power* – a must-watch for PR practitioners – a pop singer goes for an interview with a music journalist. He is with what he calls his "media mummy" – the PR consultant. The client doesn't always say the right things – not least because he is a druggie – so the consultant periodically interjects to keep her client on track.

Fourth, invite a journalist to chair, speak at or attend a prestigious event which is not directly a pitch for your products. It could perhaps be something that you are sponsoring. Never offer them money for doing this, though you could offer to make a donation to a charity of their choice.

Fifth, interact with journalists on social media. I come across media relations managers with abandoned Twitter accounts, which they haven't used for a year or two. This is a terrible sign. It implies two things to me: they aren't consuming much media, because if they were, they would get excited by some of it and share a link on Twitter. Second, they are failing to interact online with any journalists or opinion formers in their sector. Now, it may be that they are old-school and lunching the press every day, but somehow I doubt it.

Social media is personal, and therefore it is better for PR practitioners to use their real names on Twitter than hide behind some anonymous department name.

How to get the best results when emailing the press

Did you know that the time you send an email will affect the response? You would not believe how many emails get sent to journalists at 5:20pm on a Friday afternoon, when they are frantically trying to meet a deadline and thinking about the weekend.

The best time depends upon the publication. Let's say it's Tuesday and you are tapping out an email to the editor. You know that it goes to press on the same day. So today is really a bad day to be emailing the editor because it's his busiest. What should you do?

Well, there is a wonderful facility in Microsoft Outlook for Windows called "Delay Delivery". On any email you type, you can choose that option and set it to send after a certain time, say not before Thursday at 10am. The first time Outlook checks your email messages after that time, your email will be sent. In Google Mail, you can add an extension called Boomerang which similarly delays emails.

This feature is particularly useful for those who like to get some work done at the weekend. Emails received out of office hours don't tend to get much attention. I routinely type emails at the weekend and get them to send on the Tuesday.

Likewise, if you are sending press releases through an email list system such as GetResponse or Aweber, you can schedule the message to be sent at a time you think will be most effective.

Research by MailChimp found that Tuesday to Thursday are the best days of the week to email, because a higher percentage of emails are opened on those days.[48]

Every journalist is different – and every desk on a newspaper is different – but I have found that 10am until 11am is a golden hour for the national press. If a journalist arrives at the paper

---

[48] http://kb.mailchimp.com/article/when-is-the-best-time-to-send-emails.

somewhere between 9am and 10am, he will then spend some time prior to 11am reading all the stuff that has happened overnight. He starts making plans for the following day's paper. He, or his boss, might need to go into an editorial meeting at 11am or 11:30am, where decisions are taken.

The worst time to contact most newspaper journalists is late afternoon, when they are trying to write their articles for the following day's paper and are much less keen on taking phone calls or dealing with emails. By the way, I hate leaving telephone messages for journalists: not all bother to listen to them, but if they do and you call again, it looks like you are pestering. Journalists find listening to them time-consuming and therefore annoying. A.J. Jacobs, the Editor at Large of *Esquire*, says: "I'd rather get almost any other type of message than voicemail – email, text, telegram, telex, cuneiform tablet. At least you can skim those."[49] Or, as one newspaper journalist told me while listening to a barrage of mobile phone voicemails: "Why does everyone choose to talk to me on voicemail when they have an extremely detailed and lengthy message?"

It is worth asking journalists whenever you meet them what times of the day and week are busiest for them and when in the week they are keenest for stories. The information will be invaluable.

---

[49] "Is it *Ever* OK to Leave Voicemail Anymore?", http://gizmodo.com/5762401/when-is-it-ok-to-leave-voicemail (accessed March 1, 2013).

Chapter 4

How to Write an Attention-Grabbing Press Release

What makes a good press release? If you read all the nonsense spouted about them on the internet, you'd probably believe that they have to be very short, that they should start with "London, 18 November – Company today announced" and finish with "ENDS".

In fact, there are no hard-and-fast rules about laying out a press release – except that you have to grab the attention of a journalist. The old "rules" of press releases no longer apply. For example, the word "ENDS" was useful when sending a multi-page press release by fax, as it would indicate that the final page had been received. It is no longer necessary.

Starting a press release containing domestic news with the city and date – known as a dateline – is pointless in an email, because it takes up space on a journalist's computer screen which could be used for words that are actually interesting. Besides, all emails are stamped with the time and date anyway. The dateline predates the press release, and was used, from the 19th century onwards, by *The New York Times* and other papers at the start of news stories from other cities. Outside of wire services and American newspaper reports of foreign news, it is archaic.

But the genuinely pernicious myth is that press releases must be short. In fact, 27,600 websites contained the phrase "press releases should be short" when I Google-searched it during the writing of this book. This ludicrous advice is one of the reasons why PR campaigns fail.

The case for length

It is certainly true that some press releases ought to be short. But many – if not most – should be long. After all, if a story is so unimportant that the PR representative cannot find more than a couple of hundred words to say about it, should it be issued in the first place? Short press releases often go hand-in-hand with ideas that lack any weight.

The most effective media operators routinely issue press releases that, in the old days of paper, would have taken up two to four pages of one-and-a-half-spaced text. For example, I took a random Apple press release advertising a new product from its website: it came to 1,296 words.[50] Even a new staff appointment press release from BP taken at random came to 726 words.[51]

People say to me: why would a journalist want to wade through 900 words, when it could be condensed into 300? That's a good question. But think of what happens on the first two occasions when a journalist is likely to read your release. The first is when it appears in his inbox. If he is busy, he will not want to

---

[50] Apple Press Info, http://www.apple.com/pr/library/2012/10/23Apple -Introduces-iPad-mini.html (accessed February 23, 2013).

[51] BP Press Releases, http://www.bp.com/genericarticle.do?categoryId=2012968 &contentId=7080802 (accessed February 23, 2013).

read the whole release, just ascertain whether it is a potential story.

Journalists are used to skim-reading. As part of their job, they tend to read every issue of all the publications relevant to their brief. Of course, they would have no time to write themselves if they read every word of every article. Instead, they get used to reading the headlines and the first sentences or first paragraphs. And so they will try to do the same with your press release.

The question is this: is your story understandable from the headline and first sentence? The length of the rest of it, at this point, is irrelevant.

The second occasion he will read your release, he will make a proper decision about whether to write about your story. He will read the full thing and try to assess whether it "stands up" and is as interesting as he suspected. If you have only written 300 words, you will struggle to sell it to him. He will think: "How will I write a 450-word news story about this? There isn't much to it."

The inverted pyramid

The conventional way a news story is written is using a structure called the "inverted pyramid". This is also how effective press releases are written. So what is this upside-down pyramid? Well, it just means that the weighty, most important information is at the top, and the lighter, less important facts are underneath. It allows the journalist to stop reading part-way through and still understand what the story is about.

Traditionally, a press release incorporates the who, what, when, where and why of the story. That is:

- *Who* is it about?
- *What* happened?
- *When* did it take place?
- *Where* did it occur?
- *Why* did it happen?

Let's look at a good press release from Dyson,[52] which follows this design. The headline explains substance of the story:

> Dyson doubles number of UK engineers

It starts with the *when, who* and *what*. The *who* and *what* should always be in the first sentence:

> From April 2010, Dyson is doubling its UK engineering team from 350 to 700. Bucking the trend, Dyson is increasing research and development investment and recruiting during recession.

Next we get the *where,* with more of the *what*:

> The new engineers, many from university, will work at Dyson's Wiltshire laboratories, where machines are conceived, researched and designed. New positions include graduate design engineers, mechanical engineers and acoustic engineers.

[52] Dyson Press Centre, http://content.dyson.co.uk/press/pressrelease.asp?ReleaseID=76 (accessed February 23, 2013).

Later on, we get the *why*:

James Dyson said: "I am extremely proud of the new technology developed by our engineers in Malmesbury. It is vital that Dyson – and the UK – continues to invest in the nation's engineering talent if we are to stay ahead."

If you follow that sort of structure, you're on the right path.

Why newspaper standards matter

Press releases frequently fail to secure coverage because they do not hold themselves to the same standards of accuracy as would be required of a newspaper reporter.

According to Edward Bernays:[53]

The writing must be good, in the particular sense in which each newspaper considers a story well written.

In brief, the material must come to the editorial desk as carefully prepared and accurately verified as if the editor himself had assigned a special reporter to secure and write the facts. Only by presenting his news in such form and in such a matter can the counsel on public relations hope to retain, in the case of the newspaper, the most valuable thing he possesses – the editor's faith and trust.

Some deliberately attempt to mislead the media in their press releases. A common example is the opinion poll, which has been

---

[53] Bernays, op cit, p. 190–91.

conducted only once. The release claims that the poll shows that something is "increasing", where there is in fact no previous poll to compare the findings with. As Charles J. Rosebault wrote in *The New York Times* over 90 years ago: "Newspaper editors are the most suspicious and cynical of mortals but they are as quick to discern the truth as to detect the falsehood."[54]

A journalist on a British paper told me of an occasion when she was geared up to write a major story. A press release and its accompanying report made the astounding – and therefore newsworthy – claim that a majority of opinion formers in a particular sector that is controlled by the state now favoured privatisation. The reporter, however, wanted to check who these opinion formers were. She found that the author of the research had mostly asked people whose pro-privatisation views were already well-known. In other words, the research seemed to be rigged. She spiked the story.

The problem of corporate waffle

Just as important as getting the structure correct is using the right sort of language. Ray Eldon Hiebert, in his 1966 biography of Ivy Lee, writes:

> The most important attribute of any man who worked for Lee was the ability to write with simplicity and clarity. He had shelves of dictionaries and encyclopedias as well as books on writing techniques and texts on semantics. Whenever a new man would join the firm, he was given two books: Sir Arthur Quiller-Couch's *On the Art of Writing*, specifically for the chapter "On Jargon," and Havelock Ellis's *Dance of Life*, for its chapter on expression.

---

[54] "Men who wield the spotlight" by Charles J. Rosebault, in *Times Book Review and Magazine*, January 1, 1922.

Although his staff writers were excellent, Lee could usually improve any copy which he went over with his editor's pencil, and he was appreciative when associates edited his own copy. In the end, the printed material that went out of his office had a clarity, simplicity, and polish that seemed to have been achieved effortlessly because of its smoothness, but actually had involved much intense labour in preparation.

Personally, I swear by Sir Harold Evans's *Essential English for Journalists, Editors and Writers,* and Fowler's *Modern English Usage.* I wish that both of these were more commonly read by PR practitioners, as putting their linguistic advice into practice would help to improve the reputation of the PR industry among members of the press.

Corporate waffle, especially at the opening of a press release, kills a journalist's attention. One company issues releases that clog up their first sentences with boasts such as that they are "the world's leading provider of quality of daily life solutions". There is no such thing. They are a catering company.

The same firm's American unit issued a press release which stated that:[55]

> Sodexo's mobile recruitment strategy was recognised by two organisations for its forward thinking approaches to talent acquisition in an increasingly competitive labor market, and its pioneering adoption of innovation and technology to attract and retain diverse, top talent in an increasingly mobile, digital world.

[55] Sodexo Press Release, http://www.justmeans.com/press-releases/Sodexos -Mobile-Recruitment-Strategy-Recognized-with-Multiple-Awards/10822.html (accessed February 23, 2013).

Such clichéd corporate diarrhoea damages the chances of press coverage. Unfortunately, in the PR world, it is endemic. If colleagues try to force you to send out releases containing it, show them this page.

Sadly, there are times when the language used renders the entire press release incomprehensible. Here's one from Adobe, a brilliant company whose products I have reviewed favourably:[56]

> European Enterprises Need to Rethink their Collaboration Methods
>
> London, UK – 10th Feb 2009 – Adobe Systems today announced the results of a European commissioned study conducted by Forrester Consulting on behalf of Adobe to gain insight into the nature, the methods and the perceived limitations of collaborative work among European knowledge workers. Study results show that despite the pervasive collaboration trend, current tools are not meeting knowledge workers' need to work efficiently, confidently and securely together in their efforts to produce high-impact deliverables.

As far I can tell, no media outlet anywhere covered it. This is a pity, because what I think Adobe was trying to say is that we'd all be better off if we used video conferencing, but that most of the available software is rubbish.

There's a lot that's wrong with this release.

---

[56] Adobe Press Release, http://blogit.realwire.com/?ReleaseID=11261 (accessed February 23, 2013).

The headline is weak. The word "European" should not be there: there are almost no pan-European newspapers. (Quite what they were thinking when they decided to push research covering the whole of Europe, rather than individual countries, I do not know.)

Jargon is everywhere. It speaks of "enterprises", when normal people talk of companies. "Need to rethink" makes it sound like whatever is being proposed hasn't been thought through. And talk of "collaboration methods" should never appear in a press release.

Have you ever had a conversion with someone in the pub in which you've talked about "collaboration methods"? Nor have I. It is an awkward phrase that the public never use.

What the headline should be saying is "British companies lose £1 billion a year from unnecessary staff travel, says research", before explaining how video conferencing, online whiteboards and Twitter would save money.

By the way, it is vital that you say explicitly what you are in favour of.

This press release never, anywhere in the full version of it, names what it wants people to choose. Instead, it says that IT experts should "select and develop enabling solutions to satisfy enterprises' business needs and meet knowledge workers' demands". I have no idea what they mean by "enabling technologies". Do they mean Facebook?

If they do, they should say so, as it would make the story a lot less opaque.

No journalist wants to know that the "commissioned study [was] conducted by Forrester Consulting on behalf of Adobe" in the first sentence. He wants to know what the research says.

Some PR managers in large companies try to avoid sending press releases at all, given that there are so many layers of bureaucracy that want to translate their impeccable English into corporate gibberish. Instead, they simply send emails written in plain language. That's not a bad idea, even if you are not surrounded by idiots.

Effective headlines

A successful headline provides a "relevant abruption", to use a term coined by the advertising creative Steve Harrison.[57] By abruption, I mean it says something dramatic which breaks away from the banal content that fills much of what is sent to journalists. By relevant, I mean that it refers closely to the content beneath it. There's no point in using a killer headline that grabs attention, only to disappoint the readers by providing body text that doesn't meet expectations.

As Steve Harrison himself says: "It is no good, however, if all it gains is your prospect's attention. For example, setting 'BULLSHIT' [in big text] . . . will undoubtedly get you noticed. But unless you're actually in the agricultural fertiliser business . . . you'll just irritate your audience and, in turn, make them think less of the brand whose reputation you are trying to promote."

---

[57] Steve Harrison, *How to do Better Creative Work* (Pearson Education: Harlow, 2009), p. 67.

Press releases with no real story

People are naturally interested in what they are doing. So they often assume that other people are fascinated by the same things. The result is as I mentioned in Chapter 1: lots of press releases in which people bore their readers with the minutiae of their own products, without genuinely creating a story. Here's one:[58]

Kitchen Magic's acrylic doors coming soon!

With a wealth of options, finishes and design features, Kitchen Magic's extensive refurbishment ranges are already great value. But to give their customers even greater choice, the UK's leading kitchen refurbishment company is introducing a new line of acrylic doors for 2013.

"Our gorgeous new acrylic doors mean that our customers can choose from even more options, so that they really can have the kitchen of their dreams," comments Marketing Manager Samantha Davies. "These beautiful doors combine elegance and practicality, and are the perfect choice for a modern, ultra-chic kitchen design," she adds.

When I Google searched for acrylic kitchen doors, there seemed to be lots of other companies selling such things. There is no story here.

---

[58] Kitchen Magic Press Release, http://www.realwire.com/releases/Kitchen -Magics-Acrylic-Doors-Coming-Soon (accessed February 23, 2013).

What if the press release delivers bad news?

For publicly traded companies, there are times when a press release has to deliver bad news, such as redundancies. The correct thing to do is to be honest and open, rather than try to hide the bad news.

One press release which generated much criticism was issued by Citigroup[59] and was headlined:

> Citigroup Announces Repositioning Actions to Further Reduce Expenses and Improve Efficiency

Sounds positive, but no press release should be that vague. The first two paragraphs say:

> Citigroup today announced a series of repositioning actions that will further reduce expenses and improve efficiency across the company while maintaining Citi's unique capabilities to serve clients, especially in the emerging markets. These actions will result in increased business efficiency, streamlined operations and an optimised consumer footprint across geographies.
>
> Michael Corbat, Citi's Chief Executive Officer, said: "These actions are logical next steps in Citi's transformation. While we are committed to – and our strategy continues to leverage – our unparalleled global network and footprint, we have identified areas and products where our scale does not provide for meaningful returns. And we will further increase our operating efficiency by reducing excess capacity and expenses, whether they center on technology, real estate or simplifying our operations."

---

[59] Citigroup News, http://www.citigroup.com/citi/news/2012/121205a.htm (accessed February 23, 2013).

What this press release is actually saying is that they are laying off 11,000 employees. This message, however, does not appear until the end of the third paragraph, after more than 200 words. What is appalling about this press release is that nowhere in it does the boss express any regret whatsoever about the lay-offs.

Ironically, the news coverage went big on the job losses. *The Guardian's* article was titled "Citigroup to cut 11,000 jobs world-wide under new chief executive",[60] while *USA Today* ran with "Citigroup slashes 11,000 jobs".[61] *Forbes* used: "The Citigroup Bloodbath: New CEO Cuts 11,000 Jobs".[62]

If the attempt was to make the job losses less of a story, it most definitely failed. As a way of making employees feel valued, it was awful.

How to take and issue photographs

Online publishing has freed publishers from the space constraints of print editions. The result is that good photography is more in demand than ever. It is now feasible to have a picture with even a short online news story about your company, whereas in print days a magazine or newspaper might only use a picture to accompany the very longest reports.

---

[60] The Guardian, http://www.guardian.co.uk/business/2012/dec/05/citigroup -cuts-11000-jobs-worldwide (accessed February 26, 2013).

[61] USA Today, http://www.usatoday.com/story/money/2012/12/05/citi-cuts -11k-jobs/1747897/ (accessed February 26, 2013).

[62] Forbes, http://www.forbes.com/sites/nathanvardi/2012/12/05/the-citigroup -bloodbath-new-ceo-cuts-11000-jobs/ (accessed February 26, 2013).

The most important thing to remember is that photography should be of a professional standard. It is always a mistake to go to the supermarket, buy a cheap digital camera and take a few snaps yourself. Publications like stunning photographs. Besides, it's better for you if the picture of your CEO is flattering and lights his face properly, rather than making him look weird and shifty in the shadows. According to Matthew Fearn, Picture Editor of *The Daily Telegraph*: "People say that everyone is a photographer now. They're not. Unless it is breaking news, if the quality is poor it won't stand a chance."[63] Professional photographers, with greater expertise and better kit, will be able, consistently, to take images of a magazine and newspaper quality.

So how do you find a good photographer? There are plenty of freelance press photographers about, and – strange as it may sound – you may find that impoverished landscape photographers are a good choice, as they understand light exceptionally well.

Photographers will use a couple of tricks to get the right sort of photographs. Usually, the photographs that work well in news media are produced using a wide-angle lens. They let the photographer get extremely close to the subject, which produces photographs where the action is right in the foreground, creating an exciting, energetic feel.

If the photographer is taking a headshot, he will need a portrait lens: this compresses the face and gives a flattering picture. You will need head-and-shoulders photographs of all the people likely to comment to the media. They will be used regularly, but

---

[63] "The rising power of the image" in *PRWeek*, March 1, 2013, p. 25.

my advice would be not to rely on them. If you can have a stock of more interesting shots – those taken with the wide-angle lens – you will be able to provide the media with something more appealing. Journalists have seen thousands of headshot photographs, and they can be a little bit boring. What's more, many news sites like to place a photograph at the top of an article, taking up the full width of a story. That means they want a photo that's "landscape" in format, rather than "portrait" – which, unsurprisingly, is the usual shape of a portrait photograph.

If taking pictures in fast-paced or dark settings – for example, an awards ceremony, where the lights are dim – your photographer will need a fast lens (technically speaking, that is one with a wide aperture). This will mean the photographs come out well, often without the need for flash, which can be disruptive and cause people to blink. A useful guide to the subject is Professor Ken Kobré's book, *Photojournalism: The Professionals' Approach*.

By the way, attaching photos to an email clogs up inboxes, so a better approach is to upload them to a private part of your website and include a link at the bottom of the press release. Alternatively there are services that will host your images, such as Flickr and Picasa Web Albums. For use in print publications, the images need to be 300 dots per inch – or "hi-res". An image intended for web use won't do, as it will appear pixelated in print, even if it seems smooth on a computer screen.

Photographs for report covers

If you are issuing research publications along with your press releases, you will probably want to use some form of photograph for the covers. Please avoid clichéd corporate shots, especially of executives shaking hands. If you're licensing an image from a major library, you'll often get to choose whether you want a "creative" image or an editorial picture. Go for the latter, if they will let you licence it, and not only will the image be more interesting, it will appeal more to the press.

After all, the best photographs look natural, rather than posed – as though the people in the photo were not aware of the existence of a camera. Journalists spend their time with press photographs, which aren't staged.

By the way, most men like looking at women, and most women like looking at other women. That's why men's mags tend to have women on the front and women's mags are the same. This is worth considering when licensing images.

Press conferences

For most companies, press conferences should be avoided. There are certain product launches or announcements where a press conference works. They involve stories in which every relevant journalist *has* to cover the story. Manchester United, for example, can get a journalist from each news organisation that has soccer coverage to attend.

That is, alas, not the case for the majority of companies. Most journalists find themselves tied down to their desk, and travelling across a city to come to get information that could just be written in a press release wastes their time. I once went to a press conference attended by only two journalists. This sort of attendance looks embarrassing – even if the participants are the most important journalists you want to communicate with.

Elisabeth Lewis-Jones is one of many practitioners who has cut back on press conferences. She talks about when she first started working in PR in a blog post: "I worked in-house at Birmingham Airport. We regularly held press conferences and a variety of local, regional, business, trade publications and broadcast journalists would attend. I actually can't remember the last time I organised a press conference – the media just don't have the time or the resources to attend."[64]

It may be that ditching the word "conference" fixes the problem, or instead just meeting journalists one-on-one. When I reviewed Apple's Aperture photo software for a computing magazine, the technology firm flew me out to Munich to their European HQ for a demonstration. I attended with a small group of other journalists, from various European countries. It was not a press conference *per se*, and, as I understood it, other journalists were being shown the software on different days. So the fact that only half a dozen of us attended was not unexpected. The firm wanted to demo it to the press before letting us use it on our own computers so that we all understood the important features and how they worked. It was a smart strategy.

However, even when an announcement merits a press conference, it can go badly. I went to a press conference along with a *Guardian* journalist. He was hostile to what the company hosting the event was doing, and his questions were heard by all those present. The result was that every journalist listened to both the favourable angle the company the company wanted to project and to a more critical view, too.

---

[64] "Churnalism", PR Voice blog, http://web.archive.org/web/20080609071332/ prvoice.typepad.com/pr_voice/2008/02/churnalism.html (accessed February 27, 2013).

Why you should avoid sending attachments

Lots of people send their press releases as attachments. Lots of those releases remain unread.

Your press releases will get read in more haste and on more basic equipment than you might realise when you're sending them. There are still people who have primitive BlackBerrys, and they may read your release using one under the table in an editorial meeting. A PDF or Microsoft Word document just complicates matters for them. I know, I know, your boss or client wants you to include your company and trade association logos in some complicated design that you can only do easily in Word, but this won't actually help you get coverage.

The best way to send a release is in the body of an email. The subject line should normally contain the headline. Don't use the words "press release" in the subject: it will just take up space on the screen. By the way, I don't buy the argument – put forward by some PR commentators – that the press release has to be renamed a "news release", to account for TV, radio and online media. It's been called a press release since its invention in 1906 by Ivy Lee, and the term is part of the media's traditions. If we were going to rename it, the time to do this would have been in 1920, when KDKA in Pittsburgh, Pennsylvania, became the world's first licensed radio station. Besides, I've been in too many BBC studios where producers refer to a "press release" to think it is out of place. Maybe the terminology will change over time – but it hasn't yet, and – today – everyone knows what a press release means.

All press releases should be addressed to an individual journalist. It is bad form to "blind carbon copy" (BCC) a distribution list. This suggests to the recipients that they are being spammed along with hundreds of others. They will therefore consider the message less seriously than a personal email.

In fact, it is increasingly dangerous for the PR practitioner to spam hundreds of inappropriate journalists. Some news organisations have moved their staff on to software, such as Google Mail, which has a "report spam" button. If lots of journalists use this on your press releases, you might find that your future ones – including to other reporters – are automatically spam filtered. There have also been occasions when IT departments at media organisations have blocked all incoming mails from a specific domain name. Moreover, 55 per cent of individual journalists have blocked a sender of press releases.[65]

If you don't have a relationship with a journalist – and even if you do – I would include a short two- or three-line note at the top of the message, starting with "Dear Alice". By doing that you are indicating that you are not a spammer, but someone who has genuinely thought about the journalist. However, avoid the behaviour of brain-dead PR flacks who start their emails with "Hiya" and end with kisses (xxx).

Customised press releases

It is often a good idea to produce more than one version of a particular press release, so that each publication or set of publications receives news that is relevant. You will recall earlier in this

---

[65] Press Release Irrelevance Survey Findings, January 2010, http://inconvenient prtruth.com/wp-content/uploads/2010/01/An-Inconvenient-PR-Truth -Survey-Report-Final2.pdf (accessed March 1, 2013).

chapter the Adobe Systems press release which talked about "European knowledge workers". That release was ill-conceived not just because it talked in corporate-speak, but because it failed to recognise that few media outlets are pan-European. A Dutch newspaper, for example, wants to know what people in the Netherlands think.

If you are aiming for local newspaper coverage, each area most definitely needs its own release. Local newspaper journalists find it irritating when PR people send them press releases that bang on about "the United Kingdom", when their readers buy their papers to get local news. So if you're a national or international company, how should you approach them? Well, here's part of a report from the *Eastern Daily Press*:[66]

New research reveals that Cambridge is significantly more entrepreneurial than its boat race rival.

Cambridge has a business for every 21 people, whereas Oxford lags behind with a business shared between 26 people.

The figures have been calculated by Accountz, which sells home and business accounting software.

Chairman Quentin Pain said: "Cambridge beats Oxford because the best science students in the country are attracted to its university . . ."

[66] Eastern Daily Press, http://www.edp24.co.uk/business/cambridge_beats_oxford_for_entrepreneurs_1_952364 (accessed February 26, 2013).

But this PR project did not just involve press releasing the papers in East Anglia: versions of the story appeared in papers all over the country, even on the Orkney Islands. Here's what *Scilly Today* wrote:[67]

Figures calculated by Accountz, a software firm, show that Scilly is more entrepreneurial than London – and, in fact, the most entrepreneurial place in Britain . . .

Quentin Pain, Chairman of Accountz, says the Isles of Scilly is a hotbed of entrepreneurs and family businesses and he says its residents should be "proud of their contribution to Britain's economy."

These stories were based on a calculation that used government figures – creating a fun story at low cost.

"Did you get my press release?"

There is never an excuse for ringing a newspaper or magazine and asking if they received your press release. It is a telltale sign of an amateur PR practitioner – and journalists find it incredibly annoying. You won't necessarily get an informed answer. As the American journalist, Todd Wasserman, wrote on Twitter: "If I get a call asking if I received so and so, I always say yes just to rush the person off the phone."[68]

---

[67] Sicily Today, http://www.scillytoday.com/2011/07/06/scilly-most-entrepreneurial-place-in-britain-says-new-survey/ (accessed February 26, 2013).

[68] http://www.alexsingleton.com/did-you-get-my-press-release/.

There are only two times when you should ring a journalist after sending a press release. One is where you are genuinely able to offer something extra, such as an interview with a chief executive. The second is when you have offered the story as an exclusive, and you are ringing to see if they want it. It is fine to offer, but not to pester or bully.

No one enjoys making needless nagging phone calls to journalists, so why not spend your time instead with a pot of tea, coming up with some decent new ideas for future press releases?

Alas, many of those amateur practitioners believe that if they put pressure on a reporter to cover their story, it is more likely to gain coverage. They would do well to remember the words of Ivy Lee[69]:

> I know the editors of many newspapers; editors and reporters. I never ask them to print anything in their papers. In the first place, I think it is very bad business, very poor policy on the part of anyone to make such a request; and furthermore, I always feel that if I did make it, and the papers printed a story or article at my request – which they would not have printed if I had not asked them to – the people would not read it.
>
> Editors of newspapers print what they do print because they have been taught by long experience that certain things, which are said to have news value, are the items which the public will be interested to read . . . Now if the trained judgment of these men does not make them feel that a particular item will be read, what is the use of getting it printed?

---

[69] *Publicity, Some of the Things It Is and Is Not*, Ivy Lee (New York: Industries Publishing, 1925), p. 2.

Embargoes

If you are aiming for traditional media to cover your story, it is often a good idea to embargo it. This is as a courtesy to the journalist. You are giving them time to think about the story and do some research, safe in the knowledge that they will not be scooped by another media outlet that rushes it out.

Just write at the top of the press release "Embargoed until Thursday 1 May". Some people try to be clever and write that it's embargoed until "00:01 hours" – which is wholly unnecessary. Besides, first editions of newspapers are available in major cities before midnight. This is, by the way, not counted as breaking the embargo, nor is putting a story on a newspaper website in the evening. Neither will damage your ability to get coverage.

Despite setting an embargo for the Thursday, a late-night 11pm television interview on Wednesday on the subject would be fine, but an appearance on the BBC News Channel at 8:30pm would be pushing it.

While print media will almost always honour an embargo, online media may be more problematic. In 2008, Rafe Needman, then a journalist at the CNet technology news website in the United States, asserted, on a personal website, a break from journalistic tradition. He wrote that: "If you send an unsolicited email with an embargoed press release in it, we consider that fair game to cover immediately."[70]

---

[70] http://proprtips.com/2008/09/26/tip-38-presumptive-nda/.

Most journalists would be appalled by that attitude. But he may have a point. Michael Arrington, founder of TechCrunch, wrote a lengthy blog the same year explaining why his site would no longer take notice of most embargoes.[71] He explained that PR companies were sending their "embargoed news to literally everyone who writes tech news stories . . . Any blog or major media site, no matter how small or new, gets the email. It didn't used to be this way, but it's becoming more and more of a problem."

The result was that some tiny website would break the embargo, meaning that sites such as TechCrunch were at a commercial disadvantage. "A year ago embargo breaks were rare, once-a-month things," he said. "Today, nearly every embargo is broken, sometimes by a few minutes, sometimes by half a day or more."

Now, my view is that sending press releases to blogs is usually inappropriate. Many independent bloggers hate receiving press releases, regarding them as relevant to the mainstream media – or "MSM", as they call it – but not to them. Because independent bloggers are not, for the most part, paid, they don't see why they should have to deal with them. Blogs, therefore, require a more personal approach, in which emails are tailored specifically with the readers of that blog in mind – and, I'm afraid to say, you do need to read the blog. Spamming a list of carelessly chosen bloggers with embargoed press releases is asking for trouble. A trained journalist will regard an embargo as a convention that should be followed, whereas a blogger may see it is something you are asking them to follow, but something to which they have not agreed.

---

[71] http://techcrunch.com/2008/12/17/death-to-the-embargo/.

It is OK, however, to provide bloggers with embargoed information if they are bloggers who you have a relationship with, who you trust and who value you. It may be that you want them to review a product and would ideally like some reviews to be available on the day of release. Giving them the product under embargo would be beneficial to both sides.

If, given what sites like TechCrunch are now saying, you think your coverage will principally be online media, you may wish to ditch the embargo and write at the top of your press release "For immediate release". Or you could just send professional media the embargoed press release in advance, and give bloggers the information later.

In practice, in the era of 24/7 news, embargoes are less important than they once were, but they are still appreciated by most professional journalists working for newspapers, magazines and broadcasters. And they can increase the amount of coverage a story receives, because they get around the problem where a specialist correspondent is so busy on a particular day that she cannot find time straight away to think about your pitch. With a "for immediate release" story, a journalist may think that she has to write about it *right now* or not at all. If she writes about it in two days' time, she will look like she has been scooped by competitors or is lacking in her nose for news.

Giving advance notice

If you are working on a story several weeks in advance, you may gain an advantage by tipping off media planning services such as the Precise Media Planner, which – in the UK – is used by all the major news organisations from the BBC to *The Guardian*. An

Associated Press-branded version of this media planner, called AP Planner, is available in the United States. Media organisations use these media planning services regularly to ensure they know what is happening in the coming weeks.

It is also worth alerting specialist correspondents at each newspaper that a story is coming in a few weeks. Let's say your story is about how aid needs to go up to 12 per cent of GDP to pay for the cost of climate change. Ring up the environment editor or correspondent of each newspaper and let them know to expect it.

If you're a real pro, you'll try to give each paper something special. The magic words to use are: "we'd like to give you an exclusive angle". If you've done a survey, then you can tell *The Guardian*, for example: "We did a poll of 1,000 young people on their attitudes to social policy. 73 per cent of them favour legalising drugs, while 94 per cent think pubs should serve them at 16. But separately we've put together a focus group and we'd love to assemble them to be questioned exclusively by you."

Some PR campaigns do very well by meeting specialist correspondents for lunch or drinks. Political think tanks, for example, will arrange lunch with Political Editors once every year or two, a few weeks before a major report launch, while telecoms firms may well have lunch with the Telecoms Correspondent on the City desk of each newspaper.

The most important thing when arranging lunch is to have in your mind a portfolio of three ideas to give to a journalist over lunch. They want to feel that they have got some good material from you. And it helps them justify their time out of the office if they have a boss who likes to keep them on a leash.

Journalists, on the whole, don't want to have lunch with a junior press officer, so you may need to massage your job title, or consider putting someone at a senior level in front of them.

Different journalists have different deadlines, so some will be unavailable for lunch, or have earlier or later preferences. As discussed in Chapter 3, many find it difficult to get away for long periods. The worst invites are ones that involve travelling long distances. Being invited to lunch at the other end of a capital city can add an hour to lunch – and there is an increasing desk-bound culture in newspapers. So you will be best off suggesting a restaurant near to a newspaper's office.

If you're a poverty relief charity on a limited budget, don't worry. The expense you go to should fit in with the sort of organisation you are. If you're supposed to be helping starving children and you take a journalist to a restaurant with two Michelin stars, the journalist is going to think you need your head examined.

Newswires

Although I don't recommend pay-for newswire services, there are proper newswires, funded by media organisations, which are worth contacting. Indeed, newspapers and broadcasters rely heavily upon them to find and filter news. In the UK and Ireland, general news is covered by the Press Association. The equivalent in Australia and New Zealand is the Australian Associated Press (AAP). In the United States and Canada, the Associated Press and

The Canadian Press, respectively, take the lead. Reuters and Bloomberg are the main wire services about finance.

Each newswire service will provide you with details of how to submit your press release. They are, in my experience, extremely good at sorting through the material they receive by email.

Chapter 5

Dealing with Incoming Media Enquiries

The more you issue good press releases, the more your reputation with the media will grow. You will get what is called "woodwork coverage" – that is, coverage simply because you are well-known and your reputation is in the woodwork. Taking incoming media calls, which are normally extremely welcome and beneficial, does nonetheless require some skill and caution.

Incoming phone calls

I was given some useful advice when I started my first job, as a press officer in Westminster: "Never do or say anything that you wouldn't like to appear on the front page of *The Guardian*." With that parked to one side, let's examine how to deal effectively with media phone calls.

Sometimes a journalist will be struggling to find a decent organisation or person to comment on a subject. But quite often they have a choice and will be ringing down a list of possible bodies to interview or feature in some way. Therefore, it is vital that their phone calls are dealt with quickly and helpfully – which is not always what happens. Andrew Buncombe of *The Independent* says: "I cannot believe the opportunities that big companies let pass when I am seeking a comment from them on a story that is at worst neutral and at best very much in their favour. Some [public relations people] are pathetic."[72]

Allowing media calls to go through to voicemail is foolish, even out of hours. There are journalists working during evenings and at weekends. It therefore makes sense to have a media line for evening and weekend calls. Some companies have a mobile handset for incoming media calls, which they take turns to carry while the office is closed. Of course, there will be times when even this doesn't mean a journalist's call gets answered – such as when you are out of reception. You can increase the likelihood that a journalist will leave a message by recording an outgoing voicemail message saying that messages are picked up throughout every evening and weekend and that all of them are returned extremely quickly.

It is important to log the details of those journalists who ring you, as these details will be useful when you later issue press releases.

Online media centre

You will attract more incoming calls (and more coverage, even without the phone calls) by placing useful materials for the press on your website. In days gone by, PR teams would create press kits, containing useful photographs, recent press releases and background information in an attractive folder. Nowadays, these have morphed into online media centres – web pages designed for journalists.

---

[72] David Henderson, *Making News* (Nebraska: iUniverse, 2006), p. 31.

Here you should prominently list contact details for journalists to ring or email, plus give them the opportunity to enter their details in order to receive future press releases. Quite how you deal with those who leave their details will depend on the sort of stories you put out. You may want to research who the journalists are before you add them to an email list. After all, you may get competitors entering their details, along with charity campaigners who are hostile to your industry. And you may issue press releases on a variety of topics, and recognise that each press release should go to a different selection of journalists.

You may also want to deal with independent bloggers in a slightly different way to professional media, for example, by issuing an embargoed press release to professional media, and then by sending a personal email to relevant bloggers on the day of the launch. That means that addresses collected through an online media centre will need to be sorted, rather than automatically added to an email list.

Photographs of your executives and major activities should be easily downloadable from the media centre, preferably in a variety of sizes. Internet outlets will want a small image – maybe 300 pixels wide for a headshot – while print publications will need high-resolution pictures.

Finally, your past press releases should be placed in the media centre. This will help more people find you on search engines. In fact, improving your site's ranking in search engines is a good reason to host the media centre yourself, rather than paying a press release newswire to do it. It means your site gets incoming links, rather than theirs.

Unhelpful press offices

Over the past 20 years, I have witnessed a small minority of PR departments that are deeply unhelpful both to the media and to their employers. They don't return journalists' calls or they erect unnecessary roadblocks. It seems to be either a weird attempt to feel powerful or just plain cluelessness.

Here's one example of press office unhelpfulness being uncovered. Iain Dale presents a popular talk show on LBC radio, a London station with around a million listeners. He writes:

> Nine times out of ten when our producers call a government press office to ask if we could have a minister on my Sunday show, they say no. Half the time I'm sure the press officers don't even ask the ministers. The Department of Health, Home Office, Department of Education and the MoD are the worst offenders. It gets to the point when you wonder what on earth the dozens of press officers in those departments actually do all day. Every time I am turned down by the Department of Education I have a simple policy. I text Michael Gove [Secretary of State for Education]. And more often than not he texts back to say how delighted he would be to come on.

You see the disconnect there? The boss (Michael Gove) wants to appear, but his irrational subordinates don't seem to want to find this out. This is particularly odd, because Dale is himself a celebrity in Westminster. He is not someone with a reputation of unfairly stitching up guests, so the actions of those press officers is mind-boggling.

In this case, we are talking about central government press officers, and there is a specific problem in Whitehall public-sector

PR. Too many people doing it are interested in either being civil servants or in being part of politics, but are not plugged into the wider knowledge-base around public relations. I was told by the head of media at one government department that they do not spend *any* money on external training. This sentences the department to a myopic understanding of public relations.

This is despite the view of the late Sir Stephen Tallents (1884–1958), head of the Empire Marketing Board, who said that PR "should be recognised as a professional job demanding special training and special capabilities".[73] Yet I note from the job advertisements for government press officers – well, the ones I could find – that there was not even the suggestion that applicants might be a member of a professional body, or, for example, have a degree in public relations. Not even the most basic professional certificate was mentioned. This is especially odd given that there are thousands of public sector communicators who are members of the Chartered Institute of Public Relations (CIPR), an organisation originally set up by local government PR staff.[74] Currently, only one central government press office is accredited with the PRCA professional body, while a number of local government ones are. And of the 30 press officers listed on the Department of Health website as I type this,[75] not a single one is listed on the CIPR's membership register.[76]

---

[73] Sean Larkins, https://gcn.civilservice.gov.uk/blog/2013/01/07/is-pr-a-dirty -word/ (accessed March 1, 2013).

[74] Jacquie L'Etang, *Public Relations in Britain: A History of Professional Practice in the Twentieth Century* (London: Routledge, 2004), p. 57.

[75] http://mediacentre.dh.gov.uk/about/ (accessed March 7, 2013).

[76] http://www.cipr.co.uk/content/membership-networking/public-relations -register (accessed March 7, 2013).

The lack of proper PR education and training has become especially bad with the rise of special advisors – normally young party political hacks – getting involved with media relations, with often little previous experience and certainly no qualifications. The results of all this can be cringe worthy.

Commercial PR departments tend to fare better, because of the increasingly important role given to measurement and greater emphasis on training (just as in local government PR departments, too). Being helpful to the media, and securing coverage, helps commercial PR staff deliver measurable outcomes and therefore score more highly in their end-of-year reviews.

Smelling a rat or an opportunity worth avoiding

It is, of course, always important to assess whether a request for an interview, or other involvement, is a trap. If your business is in any way controversial – maybe you build wind turbines, which campaigners hate – make sure you find out exactly what the journalist's plan is. If a journalist wants to do the dirty on you, he will be extremely vague about the nature of the intended coverage, which should be a red flag. There is no shame in resisting a request for an interview until the editorial line being promoted is revealed.

If you are providing an interview with an executive, and you have the slightest worry, exchange emails with the media organisation confirming what they have told you on the phone about the scope and purpose of the interview and how long it will last. If it is for a broadcaster, ask whether there will be phone-in, where listeners can ring with questions. There is a huge difference in the amount of preparation and knowledge needed for a three-minute interview with a presenter and for an hour-long phone-in. That said, if the interviewee is confident with the subject, phone-ins can be fun. For broadcast interviews that are pre-recorded, or that will be transcribed into a written publication, you may wish to take along your own visible tape recorder, for your records. If you later feel that your words have been misquoted or taken out of context, your complaint will have ammunition.

Even where the coverage is likely to be hostile in tone, there will be times when you should participate. If there is a problem with your company or its products, engagement with an interested media is vital. If you choose not to give your side of the story, you give them considerable leeway in what they can write – some of which may be inaccurate. If you, at the very least, issue them with a written statement or written replies to their questions, you will find some or all of it is incorporated into their coverage. They will want, for legal and ethical reasons, to give you the opportunity to put your side of the story.

To apply a "tough stance" to a hostile media in more everyday circumstances, chapter 12 of *PR Today*, by Professors Morris and Goldsworthy, provides a useful guide to various techniques, all of which the authors say come with "health warnings".

Withdrawing the use of a press office

There may be times – especially if your company is controversial – that you find that a publication routinely writes negative stories about you. This can be depressing, and how you deal with it requires caution.

It is easier to do something about factually inaccurate stories than about merely hostile ones. In the UK, television stations are regulated by Ofcom (and, in the case of the BBC, by the BBC Trust). The newspapers have an Editors' Code of Conduct and an independent regulator. If a newspaper story is materially inaccurate, you may wish to submit a letter for publication, which will be covered in the next chapter, or request a correction. If the newspaper accepts that you may be in the right, they will readily accept these suggestions, as if you make a more serious complaint to the regulator, it will waste considerable time and have greater potential for embarrassment.

The best technique with hostile journalists, in the first instance, is to be as nice as you can to them – even if you do need to correct their perspective by, for example, issuing a statement on your website. Rising to the bait and denouncing them could encourage more hostile coverage at some future juncture.

Sometimes the correct response is to cut off all ties – but this has significant risks. In 2012, David Tovar, Walmart's vice president for communications, announced that "We have made a business decision not to participate in [the online publication's] articles going forward due to the one-sided reporting and unfair and unbalanced editorial decisions made by . . . reporters and editors."[77]

This was an effective strategy because the media coverage around the ban has acted as a loud rebuttal of the website's

---

[77] Eric Wemple, "Wal-Mart banishes Huffington Post", November 30, 2013 http://www.washingtonpost.com/blogs/erik-wemple/post/wal-mart -banishes-huffington-post/2012/11/30/23ffdc50-3b40-11e2-9258-ac7c78d5c680 _blog.html (accessed February 24, 2013).

criticisms. And the technique wasn't unprecedented. In 1984, Mobil Oil, fed up with coverage in a major US paper, boycotted the publication's journalists. The head of public affairs Herb Schmertz said: "We concluded that the situation couldn't get worse. We did it for our own self-respect."[78]

But it can backfire, as the act of banning a publication will often be seen as unfair in the eyes of wider public – and as an attempt to stifle debate or hide the truth. The banned publication, if it is of note, can turn the ban into a huge negative story in and of itself. There have been occasions when bans have turned a difficult relationship into a toxic one – and the chances of such consequences increases with the importance – in the eyes of the public – of the publication. A charm offensive is normally a better strategy, and this should always be deployed first.

The dangers of a hostile press are one reason why companies in the public eye retain PR consultants with crisis communications experience, who can be deployed at short notice. Often, when an unexpected crisis hits, companies with underfunded PR operations are unable to react quickly enough to the needs of media. And speed is important. That is why it is vital that social media is monitored, as this can provide an early warning of a crisis. As the phrase goes: "A lie can be halfway around the world before the truth has got its boots on."

And it is why, even when a journalist is unsympathetic to your position, banning them from your press office should be a last resort.

---

[78] Herb Schmertz, *Goodbye to the Low Profile: Art of Creative Confrontation* (London: Mercury Books, 1986).

Crisis contingency planning

All organisations in the public eye need to plan for crises. After a train crash, the PR team in the rail company concerned will need to deal with a dramatic spike in media requests and attention on social networks. Simulating how the company will deal with a range of possible crises in advance will help it to react quickly.

A good book that I can recommend is *Crisis Management: Planning for the Inevitable* by Steven Fink. It is a very practical read because the author was involved in crisis communications efforts for the Pennsylvania Governor during the Three Mile Island nuclear disaster. Similarly, the Public Relations Consultants Association runs a high-quality course on crisis communications – I participated in an excellent session led by Sheila Gunn, a former *Times* journalist who became political press secretary to Sir John Major, when he was British prime minister.

As a crisis hits, it is normally sensible to bring in external crisis communication consultants. They will help to deal with the extra workload. Because they are experienced crisis PR practitioners, they will bring experience that an in-house team may lack. And because they are independent, they will not feel as emotionally under attack as an in-house team, and will therefore be able to think in a more detached fashion. It is worth keeping a list of who you would want to work with should a crisis erupt.

Chapter 6

How to Successfully Pitch a Letter

The letters page can be one of the most-read parts of a publication. That's because readers see it as their page – one where they get to express their opinions. It is, therefore, a valuable property for public relations consultants.

The problem for PR people is that letters editors of newspapers prefer letters from normal readers, and most of the letters sent by PR flacks are worthless. But there are still plenty of letters published in the press from companies and charities, and if you can avoid sending a letter that sounds like a press release, you have a good chance of getting published.

The spirit of a letters page

For a letter to be printed, the writer needs to get into the spirit of a letters page. It needs to be written as you would speak, not how a committee of jargon-lovers would write it.

A letter saying that the government's criteria for approving drugs on the NHS are harming drug companies' profits is a self-interested letter. Letters editors are going to wonder how much the readers will care. The letter would be much more appealing if it said that "your readers who are concerned about getting the best treatment" should be worried that increased government rationing is going to stop them getting the latest drugs. This is basically the same point, but from a more reader-friendly direction.

Infuriatingly, many letters sent by bad PR companies seem to be no more than an attempt to tick boxes on their to-do lists, rather than a genuine attempt to get a letter printed. They read like recycled press releases – and probably are.

So it is vital to write the letter with the aim of informing readers, rather than as an attempt to get free publicity. Writing the letter simply to get the chief executive's name in print is a bad motivation, because you will most likely write a bad letter. However, genuinely trying to help out the readers will lead to good publicity.

The lack of naked self-interest is why charities do very well at getting their letters printed, whereas companies are often less successful, unless they are responding to a City story referencing them.

The competition

Major newspapers receive hundreds of letters per day, although they get fewer at the weekend. Older readers still write by post or fax. But the majority of letters come by email – and that's what you should use. It means that your letter will arrive more quickly and in a more convenient format.

Inevitably, many of the letters received are unprintable. They include ones about voices in readers' heads and "top secret" information about how major politicians are part of a plot by lizards to take over the world.

On a major paper it is quite likely that between 100 and 200 letters will be thought about seriously by a letters editor each day. Then perhaps 50 each day will be shortlisted. They may sit in a "queue", waiting to be used, if a space becomes available, for up to two weeks afterwards. But, normally, if they are going to be used, they will be published within two or three days. About 20–25 letters are printed each day on a typical letters page.

How a letters page is split up

Every newspaper has a formula for its page, with a mix of serious topics and lighter ones. It is good to get a feel for the types of letters that are published, as each letters page is different.

If the letters page uses a photograph, this gives the opportunity to be helpful. If you are submitting a letter, for example, lobbying for more defence expenditure, and you refer to some battle in the First World War, you could always mention in a P.S. that there is a brilliant painting of this in the Imperial War Museum (and, by the way, it's available from Getty Images). A word of caution, however: a suggestion that the paper might want to use a self-satisfied picture of your executives shaking hands will not go down as well.

What to avoid

Here's the start of a letter by Gabe Kavanagh and Rosa Campbell that was sent to *The Sydney Morning Herald*, in response to a column by Paul Sheehan. It's a near perfect example of what not to do:[79]

> We're on it, Paul.
>
> In two weeks, 400 feminists are going to argue to the death about what feminism means at the F Conference. Please come along – it can only make us stronger. Plus, your ticket's on us.
>
> The answer will be as complicated as ever – even if you don't come.
>
> When you argue that women are feminism's worst enemy, you make the same case hundreds of opinionated men and women have done before you – but you don't tell us anything new.

And so it went on for another four paragraphs. The writers complained on their blog that the letter wasn't published because (a) it was written by women and (b) by feminists.

Rubbish, if you ask me. The letter suffers from several problems. First, it is written to the wrong person. It should be written as a letter to the editor, not to the writer of the original column. Second, the readers aren't interested in whether there's a free ticket available for Mr Sheehan or not. This content is irrelevant.

---

[79]Gabe Kavanagh and Rosa Campbell, http://www.crikey.com.au/2010/03/30/how-to-get-a-letter-published-in-the-smh-1-be-a-bloke/ (accessed March 1, 2013).

Third, it's not clear to me what the original columnist was arguing, or, indeed, what the letter writers are trying to say. What do they mean by their opening line: "We're on it, Paul"? On what? The phrase "you don't tell us anything new" seems gratuitous, and the letter, taken as a whole, appears to lack an argument.

Third, the letter is advertising a conference. That will have put a quick black mark against the letter, because a letters page is for discussing ideas, and papers really don't like them to become commercials.

Fourth, it's too long. The full thing is 300 words, which for a letter that is largely vacuous, is too much. Could they not have made a point in 100 words?

The writers say that they rang the paper's letters editor to ask if it was to be published:

> The answer wasn't at all straightforward – although he did say that "at this stage, I'm leaning against publishing it".

Well, there's a tendency at newspapers not to get into a detailed discussion about why something is no good, because it just ends up causing offence. No one wants to be told that they can't write (for example).

Letters editors frequently receive calls from people complaining that their letters never appear. However, the truth is that letters don't get printed because they are not interesting or well-written enough.

If you are at a loss to understand why the letters editor doesn't like your letter, there is a magic phrase that you can use to get past the fob-off. Just say: "What could I do to make it better?" At which point, you'll often get useful advice – and maybe you'll have time to revise your letter.

One reader of *The New York Times* submitted a good, if slightly long, letter on the psychological effects of video games such as Quake and Doom. It was the sort of letter that newspapers like, because it was informative and was the opposite of the conventional video-games-are-evil position. But he did something that irritates letters editors:[80]

> I was contacted by the *Times* expressing interest in printing an edited version of my letter (I'm sure they wouldn't have printed the whole thing, it's much too long), and asking if it had been published anywhere else. I told the person I was talking to that I had published it on my personal website, and she said she'd call me back if they were still interested. She didn't, so I guess they weren't.

Some PR people will now pre-empt publication by releasing their letters to the editor in advance on their websites. This is a mistake. First, it scoops the newspaper, thereby making the letter less valuable to the paper. Second, it's impossible for the letters editor to actually edit the letter, because the writer is holding up the letter to the public and saying: this is what my letter was before this evil newspaper got their hands on it.

Normally, if the letter has been through a company's bureaucracy, it will need some editing to rid it of illiterate phrases and to get it into the style the newspaper's readers like.

I would normally be relaxed about the editing. Newspapers employ professional editors, whose job it is to make sure your letter communicates well. But, if you are worried, it's fine to ask

---

[80] http://pigsandfishes.com/natter/19990430.html (accessed March 1, 2013).

for the edited version of the letter to be emailed to you, so that you can check that your point is correctly expressed.

A correcting letter

This, from Graham Louth of the regulator Ofcom, appeared in *The Guardian*:[81]

You report that Ofcom will hold a second public consultation on proposals for 4G mobile services (Delay to 4G sale puts back smartphone revolution, 8 October). The report says that "Ofcom has decided once more to tear up its rules for the auction".

This is not the case. We have decided to hold a further public consultation to refine our proposals. This is because . . .

It's a good belt-and-braces letter, which avoids getting emotional. "This is not the case" is a wonderfully matter-of-fact phrase, which makes the point, but without making the newspaper look silly.

Too many letters of correction use aggressive words and phrases, such as "misrepresent". That particular word is legally problematic, because it could imply that the journalist has engaged in some wrongdoing. You might think that to be the case, but you'd be better off merely assuming than an honest mistake has been made.

---

[81] "Consulting on 4G" in *The Guardian*, http://www.guardian.co.uk/media/2011/oct/14/consulting-on-4g-ofcom (accessed March 1, 2013).

Furthermore, it's important to avoid being strident. Some companies attempt to rebut legitimate concerns about their practices by sending heavy-handed letters that infuriate the readers, and cause days of letters in response. Always sound reasonable and caring, and you'll do much better.

The position letter

Here's one from me, published in February 1999 in *The Independent*:[82]

> Serious economists, as well as pop stars (report, 11 February), have supported Jubilee 2000, and urged the cancellation of Third World debt.
>
> At the Adam Smith Institute, we have expressed the view that this debt burden is holding back development. These were often ill-considered loans lent by ill-advised banks to illegitimate governments. The capital is gone, in most cases wasted, and repayment comes from what little income these countries generate.
>
> By cancelling that debt on a one-off basis, we not only raise the living standards of the desperately poor, but we give them the chance, and the investment, to embark on that upward path which generates growth, wealth and jobs.
>
> Cancellation is in our interest as well as theirs.
>
> ALEX SINGLETON
>
> Adam Smith Institute
>
> London SW1

---

[82] http://www.independent.co.uk/arts-entertainment/letter-cancel-those-debts-1070193.html (accessed March 1, 2003).

The reason this works is, first, because it is unexpected. The conventional view was that do-gooders were in favour of debt cancellation, whereas free-marketers were against. So publishing a letter setting out an unconventional position was appealing to the letters editor.

Second, the letter has a neat turn of phrase: "ill-considered loans lent by ill-advised banks to illegitimate governments".

Third, it has an argument that wasn't heard much back then: "Cancellation is in our interest as well as theirs."

If I were writing it today, I would change the tense from "have urged" to "are urging" and "we have expressed the view" to "we take the view". Using the present tense sounds more current and is therefore more powerful.

The informative letter

This, from *The Scotsman*, was a brilliant letter, not just because it's to the point, but because it informs readers about something that isn't commonly known. Certainly, I had never heard this argument before:

I was astonished that Scottish Socialist Party spokesman Colin Fox didn't appear to know that VAT on domestic fuel is only 5 per cent (not 20 per cent).

Perhaps he and others who wring their hands over what they see as an outrageous rise in fuel costs also do not know that official statistics show that, in 2009, fuel expenditure as a percentage of total household expenditure was 4.7 per cent.

> That is only slightly higher than it was in 1990 (4.5 per cent)
> and less than it was in 1980 (5.6 per cent).
>
> Steuart Campbell
>
> Edinburgh

This sort of letter appeals to letters editors because the use of figures makes it sound authoritative. It is quite common on letters desks for editors to wonder: "Is this letter credible? Is it true?" Sometimes letters editors will try to verify them, particularly if the letter is disputing someone else's claims. It helps, therefore, if you footnote your letter with an explanation of where the figures came from, and include a web link, if available. This won't be printed in the paper, but it will put the letters editor's mind at rest.

The anonymous letter

Newspapers – the high circulation ones, anyway – hate anonymous letters. They look fake, and newspapers take the view that if someone wants to throw stones in a letter, he should have the courage to put his name on it. (The exception are letters in the troubleshooting columns of personal finance sections, where, for obvious reasons, names are often ditched.)

It's a bit different on local papers, where "Name and address supplied" is more common, and in one local paper caused the phrase "Disgusted of Tunbridge Wells" to be born. Apparently, a past editor of the *Tunbridge Wells Advertiser* was so short of letters that he asked his journalists to write some. One signed his name "Disgusted, Tunbridge Wells", creating one of the most famous phrases in the UK.

The grassroots or astroturf letter

In the United States, the word "astroturf" has come to refer to fake grassroots campaigns. And when letters editors receive huge numbers of letters that are being sent as part of an orchestrated campaign, letters editors are unimpressed. That's because all the letters invariably contain exactly the same phrases. Letters editors have numerous tales of the 200 "spontaneous" letters that each contained the likes of "[Insert your name and address here]" in the line above each writer's name and address.

Letters editors are not naive, and providing hundreds of people with cut-and-paste letters does not work. In fact, it is more effective to spend time penning a truly good letter from one person.

The group letter

One technique is the group letter by eminent people. Ring up the letters editor and say you're thinking of putting together a letter on x, and see if there is some interest. The fact that you have rung first will whet his appetite and make it more likely that the letter will appear on the shortlist when you email it to him.

The call can also be useful because he may say that he has no interest in it, and then you can either tweak the theme or offer the letter to another paper.

When you ring, a good question to ask is: when would you need it by? The letters editor may think it would fit well on a particular day. For example, it may be that he struggles to create a really strong letters page for a Monday morning, and therefore receiving your letter by Saturday would help him enormously.

After you've spoken to him, keep in touch. Send him a copy of the letter while you're still getting signatures so as to keep his interest. He might respond with a couple of suggestions for improving the letter. And he will feel that he has invested time in you, and therefore will want to print the letter.

If the content is particularly newsworthy, ring up a specialist correspondent and tell him what you've submitted. The specialist might be game for running a story announcing that "in a letter to this newspaper, thirteen eminent doctors have written calling for the government to cancel their NHS reforms" (or whatever your particular cup of tea is).

What's more, if a specialist correspondent tells a letters desk that he wants to run a story about a letter, the letter's publication is practically guaranteed. The letters editor won't spike the letter because he will want to be seen as helpful to his colleagues. And having a letter picked up by the news pages indicates that the letters page is driving the news agenda and is important. Sometimes, radio talk shows and television programmes will pick up these sorts of letters, so they can be an extremely time-effective way of raising profile for an issue.

Oh, and if you want the best possible chance of getting your letter printed, send it to a Sunday newspaper. These get fewer letters than daily papers. That's because readers have far more interesting things to do on a Sunday than sit at their computers typing letters – like being nagged by their spouses or walking around the countryside. Certainly, there are few readers on a

Sunday sitting at work at 9:05am, bored out of their minds with their employment, writing to the press.

For a Sunday newspaper, you ought to get your letter submitted by Thursday lunchtime. You would be amazed at how many companies submit letters at 5:30pm on a Friday afternoon, in the belief that someone is going to come into work to edit their letter on a Saturday. By that point the page will have been finished.

With a group letter, try not to go overboard on signatories. Normally, only a few of the names will appear in the print edition, along with a message telling readers that they can see the full list online.

As a rule of thumb, I would say six to a dozen signatures is a good number (although the *Chicago Tribune* has a rule of "No more than four signatures per letter"). But it very much depends on the weight of the signatories. If you have 100 Nobel prize-winners, that is better than just six. But I wouldn't scrape around trying to get any old signatory in the hope that quantity will impress.

When to submit your letter

The best time of the day to send a letter to a daily paper is in the morning before about 10:30am, although obviously it varies from newspaper to newspaper. They letters page may well be the first section of the features and comment pages that gets designed. On one major newspaper, the letters desk has normally finished compiling the page by 1:30pm, and they need letters by 10:30am in order to start working on them.

A letter, therefore, that arrives at 3pm has almost no chance of making the next day's paper (unless it is breathtakingly stop-the-press startling). And in the afternoon, aside from proofreading the page, and reading and shortlisting hundreds of letters for the following day, the letters page staff may go off to other duties.

Letters to national newspapers should always be exclusive to one newspaper, and it helps to state that this is the case. If you put: "This letter is exclusive to *The Guardian*" at the bottom of your email, it will reassure the letters editor that you aren't sending a round robin.

The reason papers like exclusive letters is that the page is supposed to be a page of letters to that paper's editor, rather than a bulletin board. Although most people may just read one paper, there are plenty of individuals – for example, those reading in a library or from an office collection of papers – who will flick through two or three. And it looks poor if the letters are repeated in several newspapers.

If you are responding to an article or letter in the paper, don't sit on the task for a few days. Your chance of being published is substantially greater if you submit the letter straight away. If you are running a good PR operation, you should be able to submit a letter on the same morning that the article it refers to was published. If your organisation is too bureaucratic for that, get your organisation to change. It really makes a difference.

Getting the details right

So how do you write a good letter? Being short helps hugely. The maximum length a letters page will normally print is 250 words, and those printed tend to be in the 50–150 word range. *The New York Times* explicitly says that "Letters for publication should be no longer than 150 words, must refer to an article that has appeared within the last seven days",[83] which is a good rule of thumb across the English-speaking world.

However, while newspapers publish many letters referring to articles, they do also print some without any reference to previous newspaper content.

The best technique for writing a letter that fits in with the writing style of the page is to open up a newspaper and see how letters there are phrased. For example, you might notice that a belt-and-braces way to start a letter is:

> John Smith (report, June 20) says that there is shortage of potatoes caused by disease. Your readers might like to know that there is a variety that they can grow which is immune . . .

Here you will notice: journalist says x. Your readers y. This works well.

The most important things to include are your full contact details, namely a telephone number (including mobile) and a full postal address. In most papers, the address will not be published, but (in the UK) it allows the paper to verify your address on the electoral roll. And the phone number is vital if the paper wants

---

[83] "How to Submit a Letter to the Editor", http://www.nytimes.com/content/help/site/editorial/letters/letters.html (accessed March 1, 2013).

to confirm any edits or just check up on whether you are who you say you are.

You can help the letters editor by including the date and section of the original story to which your letter refers. If you are reading the paper on the internet, then including a link to the story at the bottom of your email can be a genuine help. After all, the paper publishes hundreds upon hundreds of stories each week, and it is quite possible that the letters editor won't have the faintest idea when and where something appeared.

PR companies often have much newer computer systems than newspapers, and this can cause problems. Journalists – used to working in software such as Adobe InCopy – do not necessarily have Microsoft Word installed on their computers, and if they do, it won't necessarily load the latest files. Many newspapers have custom-written software where emails to inboxes like the letters page go directly into the editorial systems. These systems may strip out the attachments that people send. And they don't necessarily show the complicated formatting people use in their emails – only old-school, plain text.

So sending attachments is a mistake. In fact, good email etiquette has always been to avoid sending attachments unless they are necessary, because opening them wastes the time of the recipients. On a newspaper letters desk, if the editor has to read 500 incoming emails a day, fiddling with attachments is an unwelcome addition to his workload.

Now let me mention the most hated email attachments of all. They are when the sender has written a letter, printed it out, signed it, scanned it and then emailed it to the newspaper as an image. They are, therefore, impossible to cut and paste from. So the letters editor is forced to retype the whole thing.

How often should you write?

If you do get published, pause sending letters to that paper. Papers don't like to give the impression that they only have two readers. Many have a rule that they won't print you more than once a month. Some are even stricter. The *Los Angeles Times* says "we generally do not publish more than one letter from a single person within any 90-day period".

Chapter 7

Persuade the Public with
Compelling Comment
Articles

As a PR practitioner, you'll find that you need to write articles quite often. It's why many journalists have successfully made the transition into PR – they know how to write. But it is a skill that it is vital for practically everyone in the industry to gain, regardless of background. After all, clients and employers need good-quality writing all the time. As Fraser Seitel, a leading American practitioner, points out: "The warp and woof of public relations is still: 'I'm a professional communicator. You hire me because I'm a better writer than you are.' Therefore, the fundamental bedrock skill of this field is still . . . writing."[84]

Much of the need for article writing comes from two sources. First, when specialist publications, whether online or in print, ring asking for written commentary, which may be ghost-written by a PR practitioner. Second, for so-called "brand journalism" or "content marketing", where PR people write blogs and other web articles in order to get found in search engines or be shared on social media. And, for those doing public affairs, there's a third source: comment articles in national newspapers.

---

[84] http://www.alexsingleton.com/the-bedrock-skill-of-public-relations-is-surprisingly-rare/ (accessed March 1, 2013).

For external publications, it does not matter whether the publication wants a small box of 150 words, a blog of 350, or a fully fledged 900-word opinion piece. The quality needs to be high. After all, if the publication has any self-respect, it won't want to keep commissioning pieces from people who can't write. Unfortunately, many otherwise intelligent university graduates fail to recognise that writing well for the media requires rare skill. It requires practice.

Publications are normally too polite to explain that they won't commission from a PR flack because he can't write well. They know that editing another of his submissions would take all day. Moreover, these days journalists have a pretty good idea of how popular a particular contributor's articles have been. They can see by installing Google Analytics on their website what's popular and what's not. And the number of comments left underneath an article indicate if it provoked any debate.

But there is another challenge, too. Just as many press releases have boring topics, so do many articles submitted to publications. They should never be entirely self-serving, but should raise an important point for the sector. I came across one case where a PR flack had written and then pitched an article to a range of trade publications saying that readers should buy more of his client's products. He could not see why none of the titles would publish it.

The expert position

All publications are looking for one attribute in everyone they commission commentary from. They are looking for expertise. A newspaper thinking about school choice does not want to commission "a taxpayer from Chiswick who drives a Volvo". It wants the leader of a teachers' union, or the headmaster of Wellington College, or a current or former Secretary of State for Education. In other words, the authority of the person pitching an article is vital.

Therefore, always put forward to the press someone who has the profile of an expert. That might mean reframing their role in the organisation, or changing who is presented to the media. There is not necessarily much difference between being a Campaign Director and being a Communications Director, but the former is definitely more appealing to the media. Someone who is a director is more attractive than someone who is a deputy director – no publication wishes to admit that it has accepted the B-team.

How to pitch the article

When you pitch a comment article, it helps if it links with an ongoing news story. True, some comment articles can put topics on the news agenda, rather than follow them. But that occurs less frequently. You will need to a find an appropriate "slot" in the publication, where experts who are not on the publication's payroll contribute. There is no point in pitching an article to *The Economist*. They do not have guest columnists. But *The Times* has a daily column, often written by an outsider, called Thunderer.

A quick note about terminology. In British newspapers the normal term is "comment article", while American papers call them "Op-Eds". An Op-Ed is sometimes mistakenly thought to be short for an "opinion editorial", but is actually short for "opposite the editorial page". An editorial in the UK could mean all sorts of things, but in American newspapers it has the specific meaning of a commentary written by the editorial board, which is not attributed to any individual author. It represents the official position of the newspaper. In the UK, these unsigned editorials have a different name: a "leading article", or "leader" for short.

It is best to talk with the publication, either by phone or email, before writing the article. The commissioning editor (who could have any number of actual job titles, normally the Comment Editor or the Op-Ed Editor for a newspaper) will be able to give you some pointers about the angle that will appeal to her readers. She may suggest that you include a reference to something else that has appeared recently in the publication. And she may just say that the topic is not relevant at the moment, but would be more interesting when there is a news hook later in the year.

She may try to get some idea of your credentials and whether you can write. It helps hugely if you have a back catalogue of articles already published, which you can refer to. If appropriate, you could offer to email a couple of examples.

Some people think that they should write the article first, and then pitch it to a paper. Outside of the United States, where the practice is commonplace and comment editors receive 100 unsolicited articles a day, this is a mistake. It won't be what the publication wants to publish.

For newspapers, a commissioning editor might suggest that you write it and submit it "on spec". What that means is that they aren't committing to print it. Perhaps they don't necessarily think that you will write a good enough piece, but they would like to use it if they can.

The alternative is that they might "commission" it, which means that they are basically agreeing to pay for it. In fact, the publication will assume that you, unlike a journalist, are being paid by your employer to write the piece and you should assume that you won't actually get a fee. But the terms, if used, can still give you some idea of how keen the paper is to use your work.

By seeking a commissioning editor's opinion in advance, not only will the article be better tailored to the publication, but the commissioning editor will feel some affinity with the article and be more likely to publish it. Moreover, you will be in a stronger position with colleagues within either your company (if you work in-house) or with your client (if you're in an agency). They may want you to write something that is tediously boring, because they are not used to dealing with the media. But if you can say that you spoke to the editor and she said that it needed to cover such and such, it is more difficult for people to argue with you.

When to pitch a comment article

There is no specific number of days in advance that you must pitch a comment article to a newspaper, but if you know that something is going to be in the news in advance, then suggest it to the paper up to a couple of weeks ahead. If you pitch it the day before you want it in print, you'll probably find you are too late, or that the day you have in mind is full with regular columnists.

However, if you are trying to write based on breaking news, pitching the day before publication is fine. But do it as early as possible, before 9:30am. Email is a fine way to pitch.

For a magazine, you will need to get an idea of how their deadlines work. Asking a journalist there is perfectly OK. If they are a weekly, it may be that they put the title "to bed" on a Tuesday, and each Wednesday start working on the next issue. So a Wednesday is an ideal day to pitch.

When a publication approaches you

A publication may well approach you or your client if you have a reputation as an industry leader, or if they have found examples of your blogging or other brand journalism when doing an internet search of a subject.

Let's say the publication is interested in having you write 800 words on the merits of flying cut flowers from Kenya to London, despite carbon emissions. On the phone you need to reassure the editor who's rung that you know the subject in detail. I would mention how I went out to see farmers, and visited the good-quality houses built by the companies growing the flowers, and I'd seen the school that had been purpose built for their children. And I'd say that the opponents of this trade want to steal this better lifestyle from these families and sentence them to poverty.

If you could tackle the article in several ways, ask: "Do you have an angle in mind?" The editor will then explain what he's hoping for. You then more-or-less repeat it back to her, and, if your ideas are remarkably similar to her conception of the piece, she will then commission you.

You should ask how many words she is after, and when she will need it by. And if the title is particularly high end, it is a good idea to drop in that you've previously written for *The Times* (or wherever), as it will help to reassure the commissioning editor that you are up to the job.

The most important thing of all is that deadlines aren't like deadlines in many other industries. They count. If you promise a piece by 3pm and deliver at 5:30pm, you won't get commissioned again.

Tricks for writing newspaper-quality articles

I'm going to cover some of the techniques of writing good articles. They should not only improve how you write, but also make the writing process quicker.

A good comment article has to grab people's attention right at the start. Here are some good beginnings:

> There's nothing like a great government-sponsored gravy train to make onlookers jealous. – Titania Touché, *The Grocer*[85]
>
> So Angela Merkel and Nicolas Sarkozy agree – there is a problem in the Eurozone, apparently, and something needs to be done about it. But as to what that should be, forget it. – Allister Heath, *CityAM*[86]

---

[85] "Titania takes on Pointless Portas Pilots and Citrus calamity", in The Grocer, http://www.thegrocer.co.uk/opinion/bogof/pointless-portas-pilots-and-citrus-calamity/236763.article (accessed March 1, 2013).

[86] Allister Health, http://www.cityam.com/news-and-analysis/allister-heath/politicians-fiddle-while-rome-burns (accessed October 22, 2011).

> Whatever happened to the mighty Australian Labor Party? Just three years ago, Kevin Rudd's federal Labor government was enjoying an extended honeymoon. Labor held power in every state and territory. Yet . . . – Nick Dyrenfurth, *The Australian*[87]

The last of these three examples is the easiest to copy – the writer asks a question. Questions work because you are asking the reader their opinion (even though it is a mere piece of rhetoric). This makes you sound interested in the reader, and therefore he becomes interested in your article.

Journalists have a particular dislike of excessively bubbly copy, which they always add to their mental list of bad things the PR industry is responsible for. Too much PR material starts with phrases like: "When it comes to [insert topic]" or "Whether it's the x or y, you need . . ." before turning into a fully fledged sales pitch.

Almost as important as a strong beginning is a good ending, which should land a punch. There is nothing worse than an article that fizzles out, leaving the reader feeling that the writer didn't finish it. The ending should make sure readers leave understanding the urgency of what you are saying and maybe calling them to action.

Here are some good examples:

> In the meantime, the vulnerable will continue to suffer at the hands of the very service that is supposed to help them. – Simon Heffer, *Daily Mail*[88]

[87] http://www.theaustralian.com.au/national-affairs/opinion/its-time-labor-went-back-to-the-workers/story-e6frgd0x-1226173497722 (accessed October 22, 2011).

[88] http://www.dailymail.co.uk/debate/article-2049386/The-NHS-learn-profit-isnt-dirty-word.html (accessed March 8, 2013).

I was going to suggest that it might help to listen to [Canadian pianist Glenn] Gould after taking some of his beloved Valium – but, actually, I've just tried that experiment and, no, it doesn't help. – Damian Thompson, *The Spectator*[89] (the dash, followed by "but actually", works superbly)

David Cameron may get his way next week, but the price at next year's European elections could be bloody. – Norman Tebbit, *The Daily Telegraph*[90]

The content of an article

Just like a press release, a comment article needs to have some conflict. It may be, for example, you are recommending some improvement against the status quo. But sometimes people overdo the conflict and allow the tone to go wrong. Anger is OK occasionally, but if the tone is too outraged (e.g. it uses phrases like "this is disgraceful") the readers will recoil. In fact, comment-writing is like cooking. If you use too much heat, the cake will burn on the outside, but be half-baked inside.

It is much better to keep an article feeling a bit more relaxed – indeed, jollier in tone – than come across as a raving nutter. And if you get the opportunity to gently poke fun, you'll captivate the readers.

What is essential is that your articles are not wooly and are explicit in what they are arguing. When Ernest Hemmingway – one of the greatest fiction writers of the 20th century – was a

---

[89] Damian Thompson, The Spectator, http://www.spectator.co.uk/arts/music/6649333/pillpopping-pianist/ (accessed March 1, 2013).

[90] http://www.telegraph.co.uk/news/politics/david-cameron/8838595/Europe-has-broken-leaders-before-will-Cameron-share-their-fate.html (accessed March 8, 2013).

reporter at the *Kansas City Star*, he was given a sheet of tips for writing well. This included the advice that he should "Use vigorous English". David Garfinkel,[91] former San Francisco Bureau Chief of McGraw-Hill World News, defines this as follows: "It's muscular, forceful. Vigorous English comes from passion, focus and intention."

Newspaper grammar

Go easy on the adjectives – and perhaps eliminate them entirely. PR people love them, but if overused they make text sound less convincing.

No column should contain a semi-colon – ever. Newspapers are designed to be read at speed and semi-colons create unnecessarily long sentences. Use a full stop and a start afresh. As the poet Richard Hugo put it: "Semi-colons indicate relationships that only idiots need defined by punctuation. Besides, they are ugly."[92]

Don't split an infinitive. There is nothing in the laws of grammar that says that this is wrong and to routinely split them is perfectly correct English. Indeed, it is sometime preferable, as it helps the clarity and beat of the sentence. However, like splitting the atom, it upsets campaigners. H.W. Fowler, the great authority on the English language, mocked the anti-split infinitive brigade, but the bogus rule holds sway.

---

[91] http://world-copywriting-institute.typepad.com/world_copywriting _blog/2005/03/four_copywritin.html (accessed March 1, 2013).
[92] John Henley, "The end of the line?" in The Guardian, http://www.guardian .co.uk/world/2008/apr/04/france.britishidentity (accessed March 2, 2013).

Fake rules taught at school about the supposed wrongness of prepositions at the end of sentences, or of the evil of sentences beginning with "and" and "but", can be ignored. As Winston Churchill, who worked as a journalist before a higher calling, wrote: "This is the sort of bloody nonsense up with which I will not put."

Newspapers prefer an active, rather than passive, voice. In the active voice, the thing in charge of doing stuff is the subject. For example: "The journalist turned on the computer." The passive would be "The computer was turned on by the journalist." Suddenly, eight words are used instead of six. The passive also sounds more boring.

Proofreading

Once you're written your piece, it helps to print it out in double-spaced 14pt Times New Roman text and slowly read it back to yourself – preferably aloud. Printing off a hard copy is routinely done by journalists, who can find it is easier to see problems on paper than on a screen.

This will not only help you spot typos and missing words, but also ensure that the text flows well. And if you can get a colleague to read it, too, that's even better. You may also spot stylistic problems, for example the overuse of the same word several times in a paragraph. If "employee" keeps being used, why not change one reference to "worker"? It makes for a less repetitive read.

Finally, make sure your facts are correct. It is easy to "remember" things that are almost correct, but not quite. No one at the publication will necessarily fact-check your article, as the days of hundreds of sub-editors and copy editors is over. Publications will assume that you know what you are talking about. And if the editor has to later print a letter correcting your piece, not only are you going to look silly, but you are also less likely to be used in future.

The most important word in the English language

How do you keep readers interested? One way is to make them each feel as though the article was written for them – and them alone. The simple use of the word "you" littered throughout the piece will make it seem more relevant. But the "you" should always be singular – it doesn't work as well if you start referring to "you readers".

Asking the readers a rhetorical question or two is also very effective. It will encourage comments to appear under online articles if the facility is available and, again, will keep interest.

The Flesch–Kincaid reading ease test

Before you submit an article to a publication, a useful check is to run it through the Flesch–Kincaid reading ease test. You feed your article into a mathematical analysis on your computer, and the result it gives will indicate how easy your article is to read. The higher the score, the better. The test is actually built into Microsoft Word's spelling and grammar checker, although it has to be turned on in the program's preferences. I find it quicker and easier to paste my copy into one of the websites that offer Flesch–Kincaid reading ease tests.

A study looking at popular magazines in America found that *Reader's Digest* on average scores 65 out of 100 on this test and *Time* magazine scores 52. I checked an article in *The Economist*, and found 42.

So what do those figures mean?

A score of 90–100 means that an article is easily understood by an average 11-year old. 60–70 means it is easily understood by a 13–15-year old school pupil. And below 30 means it is best understood by a university graduate.

If you're writing in a quality newspaper, you ought to always get a score of 40 or higher.

The Flesch–Kincaid reading ease test can be an effective way for PR teams to persuade others in their organisations to revise their articles. It is, after all, not a subjective view about the merits of an article, but an objective one.

Promoting the article

Once a comment article has been published, you may want to promote it yourself as widely as possible – and the publication will love you for doing so. The more hits the online version of the piece receives, and the more comments, the better. It will indicate to the publication that your work attracts the interest of the readers and that you are worth using again in the future.

Make sure you email it to whatever relevant email lists you or your organisation control – and share it on social networks such as Twitter. Your existing customers or supporters will be reassured by seeing you appear in a reputable publication: it acts as one of those third-party endorsements that are so valuable in public relations.

Dealing with rejection

You probably won't get much feedback from a publication – just a yes or no. Plenty of editors – if they weren't as polite – would love to use phrases such as one written by Hunter S. Thompson, who, working at *Rolling Stone*, sent a rejection letter[93] saying:

> You worthless, acid-sucking piece of illiterate s**t! Don't <u>ever</u> send this kind of brain-damaged swill in here again.

In fact, Thompson himself used an ingenious method of learning to write well: he placed his typewriter next to Ernest Hemmingway novels and retyped those books. And you may find that by sitting with a comment article by a major pundit and trying to see how she structured it, you will get some ideas on how to do it well.

As always, you can ask an editor: "For future reference, how could I improve this?" and if you're lucky, you'll get some constructive advice.

The problem with American newspaper columns

One reason why American city newspapers are losing readership to UK newspapers and home-grown websites is that they publish

---

[93] http://www.huffingtonpost.com/2011/08/16/hunter-s-thompson -letter_n_928491.html (accessed March 1, 2013).

too many dull columns. Tedious essays displace the lively banter that British, Australian, New Zealand and Canadian newspapers thrive on. I asked the boss of one of the most popular American news websites why this was (I had a copy of *The Washington Post* in my hand at the time) and he said that the journalists "have given up". Most of these papers, before the internet, were effectively local monopolies, and they believed that their authority came from being as formal and learned as possible. The Brits, conversely, have always had a healthy selection of national newspapers, fighting daily at the newsstand for custom.

Even William Dean Singleton (no relation), whose MediaNews firm is the fourth largest newspaper company in the United States, admits that American newspapers are "boring": "We've got to make them much more compelling than they are today. As an industry, for the last 30 years, we've edited newspapers for each other and to win awards so we could pat each other on the back."[94]

It's a point echoed by Matthew Engel, writing in *The Guardian* in 2003:[95] "Since Watergate, the [*Washington*] *Post* has acquired a virtual monopoly over the Washington newspaper market, grown fat and – frankly – journalistically flabby. Its op-ed page is notable for its turgid prose."

The problem these stuffy American newspapers cause is that many of the people doing media relations for global

---

[94] Katharine Seelye, New York Times, http://www.nytimes.com/2006/04/27/business/media/27paper.html (accessed March 1, 2013).

[95] Matthew Engel, "Bushwhacked", January 13, 2003, http://www.guardian.co.uk/media/2003/jan/13/mondaymediasection.terrorismandthemedia (accessed March 1, 2013).

organisations have learned media relations from America. Several British PR practitioners have told me of the difficulties they face when American clients send them pre-written material to place, which is unsuitable for the British press.

But the American media is changing rapidly – and becoming more British. *The Daily Mail*'s website has, in the words of the BBC, "stormed" the American news market,[96] while new American news sites from *The Huffington Post* to *The Daily Caller* have grabbed market share. The desire in the United States for interestingly presented comment is hardly surprising: America's ratings-driven television news programmes have always been livelier than heavily regulated British ones.

---

[96] BBC News, "How the Daily Mail stormed the US", http://www.bbc.co.uk/news/magazine-16746785 (accessed March 1, 2013).

Chapter 8

The Secrets of Effective Television and Radio Appearances

Appearing on television and radio is one of the most effective ways of communicating with a mass audience. The BBC's flagship *Today* programme gets 6.94 million listeners a week, while its namesake in the United States, NBC's *Today* show, gets around five million TV viewers.[97]

The emergence of 24-hour news channels, plus the enduring popularity of talk radio, means that broadcasters are in constant need of knowledgeable experts to appear as guests. But, I must say, potential guests do need to have a credible claim of expertise. The head of operations at a train company is an expert in transport. A published author, who has written a history of the America Civil War, is a history expert. And the head of an anti-poverty pressure group is plausible to talk about foreign aid. But, after the success of television programmes such as *The Apprentice* and *Dragons' Den*, lots of self-employed people decided that they were experts in entrepreneurship and pitched themselves around the media. It didn't work, because – unlike Donald Trump and Lord Sugar – they didn't appear to news organisations as having any particular expert status.

---

[97] http://mediadecoder.blogs.nytimes.com/2013/02/21/return-of-robin-roberts-brings-higher-ratings-to-good-morning-america/ (accessed March 5, 2013).

Let's say you work for a company that offers pensions to the public. You want to secure more broadcast appearances by your CEO. The simple, first task is to produce a one-sided "expert sheet". You get a box of nice paper and put the word "Expert" in big letters across the top. Underneath you put the CEO's name and position, and a selection of half a dozen bullet points about the things he is able to speak on – for example, how plans for pension regulation will strangle the industry. Then, include a paragraph on the CEO's current role and background – for example, you could mention that he was an advisor to a government commission on the future of old age. This is where you are selling him as a genuine expert. Somewhere on the page a good photograph should be included, so that television programmes know that he doesn't look weird. At the bottom of the page, include contact details through which programmes can book him.

This simple and cheap technique was effective enough to get me interviewed by BBC Two's *Newsnight* and Radio 4's *Today* programme the first time I used it.

Appearing on television

You will either appear in the same studio as the presenter or, if the main studio is too far away, in a remote studio. If you are with the presenter, you should always look at him (or the other guest). The cameras should be completely ignored. The cameramen will do their own work, but if you stare at the camera, you will look unnatural.

However, if you are in a remote studio, different rules apply. There, you look straight at the camera. There is a temptation that many people fall into. They look at the screen somewhere above or to the side of the camera, which displays how they look on television. The viewer sees them moving their eyes to look off screen. The result is that the interviewee appears shifty and untrustworthy. I know someone who fell into this trap while on prime-time British television. He was mightily upset about it, because, after the interview, people kept pointing it out to him. So never look anywhere other than the camera lens.

It is best to lean very slightly forward, rather than slouch back, as this will make you look more engaged. When someone else is speaking, turn your head slightly to one side, to indicate that you are listening. And, unless you are appearing to defend a company which has just killed a dozen people, remember to smile. It makes you look friendly and like a decent person. Moreover, it improves the sound of your voice.

This may sound obvious, but television is a visual medium. You should therefore play up to it. If another guest is saying something you disagree with, shake your head. Or raise your hand in front of your chest and wave it dismissively. Or grin, knowingly. The programme's crew will almost always change camera in response, moving from your opponent to you.

Although we live in an increasingly informal world, it is almost always correct to dress smartly for television. For women, that might mean a business suit in a solid colour. For men, it means a jacket and tie. Occasionally, I have been on television – particularly on a Sunday – where the programme has specifically wanted to avoid tie-wearing. But the tie will help to make you look thinner (if that's an issue) and also give you more authority. I once did a *BBC Breakfast* segment incredibly early in the morning, and the other guest turned up in a stained T-shirt that presumably he'd been sleeping in. *"What? I didn't know this was television!"* he said. It helped me appear the better informed.

If you don't always dress smartly in the office, for example during the hottest part of the summer, it is worth keeping a spare set of clothes in a cupboard somewhere. Finely striped patterns should be avoided on clothing. These can cause "interline twitter", which is an annoying flickering, on some televisions.

Depending on the programme and the broadcaster, you may be offered make-up. Always accept this, as it will make you look healthier under the studio lights. Moreover, if you are – how can I say this delicately? – someone plagued by spots or broken capillaries, the make-up will probably disguise all this. Most importantly, it will remove any sweaty shine that might exist on your face. Infamously, Richard Nixon was said to have lost to John F. Kennedy during the 1960 US presidential election as a result of a sweaty face during a televised debate. If the programme does not offer make-up, go into the studio's lavatory and check that you look OK in the mirror. A quick wash of the face may be just what you need.

Finally, consider that you could be being recorded even when you don't think you are. In 2010, Gordon Brown, then the British Prime Minister, still had a live wireless microphone attached to his suit when he described a voter he had just met on the campaign trail. She was, he said, a "bigoted woman" and his conversation with her had been a "disaster".[98] The gaffe dominated the news for days and became a defining episode of the election.

---

[98] How Gordon Brown "bigot" jibe row unfolded, http://news.bbc.co.uk/1/hi/uk_politics/election_2010/8649448.stm (accessed March 6, 2013).

Appearing on radio

Radio is easier than TV, because you can have a sheet of paper in front of you while you speak. I never have more than 10 words written down, and typically include a few killer figures that I don't want to forget. It would be a mistake to have a written-down speech as reading from it would make you seem wooden.

You will quite often be given much longer to speak on radio than on television. There is a different level of preparation required for a three-minute interview than for an hour-long programme. Radio phone-ins, where normal (and even abnormal) members of the public can ask you a question or dispute what you are saying, require a good debating style. Interviewees who were debaters while at university will enjoy this. Others, who are not used to debating, would benefit from first doing a mock interview, where they take part in a simulated – and deliberately difficult – interview.

As with television, I always prefer to be in the same studio as the presenter. You can catch his eye, and before the programme you can build up some personal rapport. However, I always avoid, where possible, discussing the topic of debate with another guest (assuming they are there to give an opposing view). It's much better to keep the adrenaline stored up for the debate itself, and there's no point giving out your best lines in advance.

Major broadcasters will treat you fairly. But be careful of temporary community radio stations and internet programmes – the interviewer may just want to have a go at you. You need to have a pretty good idea of their biases and proposed line of questioning before agreeing to appear.

Your own radio studio

Sometimes a radio station will be willing to do an interview, not in their own studios, but down the telephone with you. This is not ideal for them, because the sound quality of an ordinary, analogue telephone call is actually quite poor. You and I don't notice it normally, but when the interview is played on listeners' expensive hi-fi sound systems at home, it sounds awful.

Therefore, if you are putting forward staff to appear on radio regularly, and travelling to broadcasters becomes a pain, it can make sense to create your own soundproofed radio studio. This requires a small room, big enough for a desk and chair. Instead of a normal phone line, you get your telecoms company to install a digital phone connection, called an ISDN line, plus some equipment called an ISDN Reporter's Box. This squeezes really high-quality sound down the ISDN line. There are suppliers of these systems who will advise you on exactly what you need. Glensound Electronics supplies the BBC and has sold over 8,000 units. And it is worth having a chat with a studio technician when you are next at a major broadcaster, as they will be able to explain their preferences.

For pre-recorded programmes, internet-based phone calls can be used as an alternative. These occur both in their conventional form of "Voice over IP" (IP being internet protocol), which normally means Skype, and in a specific broadcast standard called Audio Contribution over IP,[99] which is gaining momentum.

---

[99] BBC Research White Paper, "Standardising Audio Contribution over IP Communications", http://downloads.bbc.co.uk/rd/pubs/whp/whp-pdf-files/WHP170.pdf (accessed March 6, 2013).

However, normal, bog-standard internet connections are generally considered to be too unreliable at present to be used safely for live broadcasts. While Audio Contribution over IP is probably the future due to the way it deals with the vagaries of internet traffic, ISDN is a standard that works reliably today.

The pre-record

Sometimes television and radio will want to interview you, on your own, to include as part of their "package". This is a short video that is played during the programme to introduce the topic to the viewers at home. A crew may be sent to your premises to do this sort of recording. Normally, the questions the interviewer asks you will not be included when clips from the interview are broadcast, but ask if this is the case before you start answering.

If the questions won't be used, then you need to answer in such a way that the topic is clear from your answer. Let's say you are asked: "Is the opening of your new factory a vindication of the government's economic policies?" You should never answer with: "Yes, very much so." That would be unusable on its own. You should answer: "The opening of our new factory shows . . ."

Pre-recorded interviews do normally allow you to fluff your lines and then answer a question a second time. Just say "Sorry, can I do that again?" The crew will take care of it in the editing process. You would have to be very unlucky, or hated, or a Cabinet minister, for the unedited interview to be broadcast. But if you are concerned about being stitched up, insist on a live interview. As Herb Schmertz, a Vice-President at Mobil Oil, wrote in 1986: "A growing number of executives refuse to be interviewed at all, unless the interview is live. That way, 'creative' editing cannot distort what they say."[100]

Don't be a robot

In a notorious pre-recorded interview with ITV's Damon Green, Ed Miliband, leader of the UK's Labour Party, answered every question he was asked with exactly the same set of soundbites.[101] Six times he said the same thing, making a recording which the interviewer described as "so absurd". It went viral on YouTube. According to Krishnan Guru-Murthy, a presenter on Channel Four News:[102]

> Somebody in political PR training school obviously told [politicians that if] you want to make sure the media only use what you want them to then only say one thing.
> Ed Miliband's crime was to deploy the technique to such a perfected degree that he looked like a robot.

Effective guests are quotable and they do ensure that their main points are incorporated, but it is important to be human.

Start off small

You may not always have the luxury of doing this, but I would also suggest putting a new talking head on a programme with

---

[100] Herb Schmertz, *Goodbye to the Low Profile: Art of Creative Confrontation* (London: Mercury Books, 1986), p. 89.

[101] http://www.guardian.co.uk/politics/2011/jul/01/ed-miliband-interviewer -shame-strike-soundbites (accessed March 5, 2013).

[102] http://www.channel4.com/news/krishnan-guru-murthy (accessed March 5, 2013).

low audience figures. This will be less stressful than a prime-time show, and if mistakes are made at least they did not happen on Comedy Central's *The Daily Show with Jon Stewart*. I think my first TV appearance was on a current affairs programme produced by a local ITV station called Grampian. It was broadcast only in central and northern Scotland, at half past midnight. Inexplicably, my boss did not want to take the seven-hour train journey from London to Aberdeen to appear in it, but I was happy for the experience – even if next to nobody watched it. The practice was invaluable for when I later appeared on highly rated shows such as *Newsnight* and *Ten O'Clock Live*.

Now, there is always the possibility that a terrible performance on a low-visibility programme will then be retransmitted in a more popular programme. But, generally, programmes with low ratings are a good way to train for the prime time.

Preparation

Never do a broadcast interview without preparation. There will be occasions when the right decision is to turn down an interview because it is about a topic that you haven't thought about for a couple of years and you don't have sufficient time to read up on the subject, or to get the latest data.

A good plan is to have three points, one of which is your key one. Don't give them all in your reply to the first question, but incorporate them into your answers as the interview progresses.

The snowball

If a guest is an effective and interesting voice in the media, there will be a snowball effect. That is to say, if *BBC Breakfast* rates his appearance, he will get put down in a programme researcher's contacts list and get invited repeatedly.

Broadcasters never seem to have a centralised database of talking heads. I did ask various people at the BBC, but there is no such thing. However, there have been occasions when I have appeared on one show and then another show contacted the first for my details.

Broadcasters often pick up on news stories that have appeared in the newspapers or on newswires (that is to say, the ones that are paid for by media organisations, not wires that send out PR spam). So if you have appeared in a morning newspaper, it is quite possible that a researcher on a programme you had not thought about will contact you, asking if you will appear as a guest. "For as long as anyone can remember", says David Henderson, a former CBS News correspondent, "it has often been the habit of television news to follow or react to major stories that first appeared in newspapers. A big story appears on the front page of a morning paper, and throughout the day and into the evening, it's recycled by television news."[103]

In fact, the relationship works both ways. A major interview on the BBC's *Today* programme may get picked up by newspapers – especially by their websites.

---

[103] David Henderson, *Making News* (Nebraska: iUniverse, 2006), p. 19.

Chapter 9

How to Choose an Agency or Consultant

If you work in-house as a PR practitioner, you may at some point want to hire a PR agency or freelance consultant to help you. Many firms prefer to use agencies or consultants, rather than manage a mushrooming in-house team. This is for three reasons. First, it gives them more flexibility. They can hire and fire a third party more easily than staff, and they can speedily increase or decrease the amount of PR support they are buying. For example, a company which hosts a yearly conference every November may need a lot of PR resources in the autumn, but much less in January. Use of an agency or independent consultant allows a firm like that to cope with a seasonal increase in media interest.

The second advantage of using agencies or independent consultants is that they enable companies to bring in specialist skills – such as crisis communications and government relations – that may only be needed, in a massive way, once a decade. Practitioners with a lifetime use of these skills might be prohibitively expensive to employ in-house.

Thirdly, agencies and independent consultants bring an extra source of ideas. After all, it's easy to become wedded to an employer's normal way of working. External staff will probably have worked on a range of clients and therefore bring a wide range of perspectives.

It is this third reason – an extra source of ideas – that most commonly causes an agency or consultant to be hired, and normally on retainer. They bring an injection of creativity. This can work so well that some in-house teams have outsourced the bulk of their media relations, becoming commissioners of agency work, while doing high-end counsel to executives themselves. This was made most apparent to me when I went to provide media-relations training to the PR team at one of the UK's largest law firms. "We don't actually deal with the media ourselves", the head of PR said. "But we want you to teach us more about media relations, so we know if our four agencies are telling us the truth or just stringing us along."

How to select an agency

I hate to say the obvious, but if you want to hire an agency on a big retainer, why not try them out on a project first? An agency may seem fantastic when its boss comes and presents an intricate PowerPoint presentation, full of diagrams containing Maslow's "hierarchy of needs" and Grunig's "two-way symmetrical public relations". But an impressive presentation does not prove that you will work together well. It is something that will only become apparent if you give them a trial before contracting with them long-term.

One company told me that it had invited three firms to pitch for a retainer. All of them had a background in the relevant sector. Two of the companies pitching displayed PowerPoint shows that

expressed no knowledge of the client. The third presented PowerPoint slides about the client. This third agency, unsurprisingly,
was the one which won the work. Unfortunately, the implemen-
tation was passed to an inexperienced staff member and the firm
did a lousy job. It failed to provide any measurable benefit and
passed off as press coverage articles that appeared on websites
where PR practitioners can upload whatever they wish. The
agency, which is not a member of a trade association, was good
at pitching, but appalling at doing.

Audit your communications first

There are many reasons why clients and agencies separate, but a
common reason why some companies keep changing agencies is
that they are not procuring them correctly. It is almost always
worth commissioning an external audit of your communications
before contacting potential agencies. This should be from an
independent consultant with no plans to tender for your agency
contract.

A communications audit will benchmark your current results
against both your direct competitors and also companies of the
same size as yours in other, but related, sectors. This will give
you a realistic view of the results an agency can achieve – and
highlight issues around your public relations that you may not
have considered. The knowledge is advantageous because during
the procurement process you will invariably find agencies that
are foolishly optimistic about what they can achieve. So you will
be in a better position to choose wisely and perhaps save yourself
a messy and time-consuming divorce.

Why trade association membership matters

If you're in the UK, make sure the agency is a member of the Public Relations Consultants Association (PRCA). There are similar, affiliated organisations around the world. The PRCA, which was founded in 1969, ensures proper standards are followed and gives you access to an independent complaints procedure. It also forbids its members from badmouthing any former clients – something that an old, finished contract is unlikely to ensure as effectively.

Almost all of the good agencies opt to join the PRCA, which includes firms of all sizes and specialisms. Partly this is because the PRCA is a major supplier of training to agencies. It gives discounts to members, so those agencies that are investing in their staff's skills almost invariably join the organisation. Moreover, agencies who, instead of wanting to make a quick buck, are thinking longer term about raising standards in the industry, join the PRCA so they can contribute to the sector's thinking.

You can ask the PRCA to match you with an appropriate agency, using its Find a PR Agency service. The association will shortlist agencies who have an appropriate size and expertise for your work. All the agencies that are recommended have passed a certification called the Communications Management Standard and have been audited within the past couple of years. What does this mean? Well, the certification is almost a hybrid of ISO 9001 and Investors in People. It indicates that a company is well run and has effective systems in place.

In the United States, the Council of PR Firms represents agencies which include "global companies and small boutiques that provide expertise to Fortune 500 companies all the way down to Main Street mom and pops".[104] You should also check out the influential trade newsletter *O'Dwyer's*, founded by a former *Chicago Tribune* reporter in 1968, which runs a Find The Right PR Agency set of listings on its website.

Both the PRCA and the Council of PR Firms are members of the International Communications Consultancy Organisation (ICCO). This global body has a website (www.iccopr.com) that lists trade bodies in many countries. Through the ICCO, the Communications Management Standard is becoming adopted in many countries – in 17 as I type this – and looks set to become a global standard.

Other considerations

First, check whether the agency has a profile within the industry. An agency which is getting coverage in *Communicate*, *CorpComms* or *O'Dwyer*'s is investing time in promoting its reputation – and is less likely to be stuck in a rut. Always be keen to give the agency credit for its efforts, and, if the work is sizeable, make sure they are associated with your company through a news story in the trade press saying that you have awarded them the contract. Suggest that they enter their work for you as an entry for one of the industry awards. This will ensure that they sweat blood to do a good job on your account, as their reputation is on the line as much as yours.

Second, once you have made a shortlist, ask to see the results of an agency's work. If your aim is to get into *GQ* magazine, what

---

[104] http://prfirms.org/.

coverage for similar companies have they managed to secure there? Most agencies will freely make available a list of their clients. If they specialise in public affairs (government relations), it is considered bad form not to disclose their clients. Indeed, it is a requirement of PRCA membership that they name their clients on the association's public affairs register.

Third, avoid those small agencies where the PR is just a bolt-on to other marketing services. In practice, this can mean that the proprietor is actually an expert in desktop publishing, logo design or internet marketing but does a bit of PR on the side. You wouldn't hire a decorator to install a new gas boiler in your home, after all, so why hire a logo designer to do PR? They may not realise that public relations needs skills and knowledge, but need them it does. A small agency that will be good at PR is one that specialises in it.

Fourth, take up references. There are some unethical agencies (outside of the PRCA or similar bodies around the world) who have no happy clients at all. But they are surprisingly convincing when signing up new ones, promising vast coverage. Usually, they keep their clients for a few months, before being sacked for non-delivery.

Ethics are important in PR, because they are the right thing to follow and because they deliver better results. According to Tom Watson, a professor of public relations at the University of Bournemouth: "Every year, a few students coming back from placements with stories of how their PR employers had misled clients, asked them to write fake customer reviews on websites, switched account teams after winning pitches, charge high for untrained internship staff and falsified evaluation data." He says that "most of the miscreants are in the 80 per cent plus of UK PR practitioners who are not members of CIPR [Chartered Institute of Public Relations] or PRCA".[105]

The staff

You will want to vet the individuals who will personally be working on your account – just as you would if you were hiring them to be a PR practitioner on your firm's payroll. Find out how long the staff seem to stay at the agency: there is nothing more disruptive, as a client, than having the people working on your PR change continually. I have seen instances of agencies at the less reputable end of the industry with "account managers" who are, in fact, unpaid, temporary interns with no previous experience.

In fact, having unpaid interns in an agency is increasingly seen as beyond the pale, after television and newspaper exposés. The Public Relations Consultants Association and *PRWeek* in the UK have campaigned against the practice of using unpaid staff for genuine work. As Francis Ingham, Director General of the PRCA says: "The short-term benefits of free labour are greatly outweighed by the way that this practice devalues our expertise and reputation. It is unfair to ask young people to work for free, just so that in the short term organisations can benefit financially. Public relations professionals provide valuable counsel and should be prepared to pay those who contribute accordingly. I

---

[105] "Does PR need to clean up its act?" in *PRMoment*, January 10, 2013, http://www.prmoment.com/1249/Does-PR-need-to-clean-up-its-act.aspx (accessed February 24, 2013).

believe passionately that we can set an example to other industries on how our young workforce should be treated."[106]

The independent consultant

Independent consultants are typically experienced practitioners who have previously worked in agencies or the media, who bring a premium and personal service to their clients. They may prefer the excitement of helping clients to the bureaucracy that inevitably comes from leading a large agency, with all the staffing and marketing hassles that such posts entail.

There are two main types of independent consultant. The first are those that act as contractors who deliver normal PR services, including writing press releases and getting coverage. They bring some external creativity into what you might be doing in-house and, for smaller companies, act as an outsourced press office. You can spot the good ones from professional body membership: they are typically members of the Chartered Institute of Public Relations.

The second are the higher-end strategists, who will help formulate and evaluate your PR efforts, provide crisis communications help, train your in-house team and ensure that you're outperforming your competitors. Strategists can also help you run your procurement process for hiring an agency, as they will have a good idea of which agencies are performing well and will know what questions to ask and what commitments should be

---

[106] PRCA Intern Guidelines, http://www.prca.org.uk/assets/files/PRCA%20 Intern%20Guidelines.pdf (accessed March 1, 2013).

requested. And they will have an encyclopaedic knowledge of what stakeholders – including the media – will find of interest.

Independent consultants tend to consider carefully which clients they take on, as they don't have to meet their shareholders' growth targets. Rather, they want clients with whom they're going to have a good relationship.

Qualifications for PR practitioners

Anyone can call him or herself a PR practitioner. As Stephen Waddington, a leading figure in the industry, says: "There is little that separates public relations practitioners from car salesmen and women, estate agents, journalists or lap dancers. All are respectable occupations to varying degrees but none require a professional qualification or any form of formal training to operate."[107] Therefore, it is worth asking a prospective agency about their staff's credentials and what commitment they have made to the professional development of their staff. Effective agencies host a regular programme of training workshops for their staff with external speakers or allocate each staff member a training budget.

Mostly, PR practitioners are university graduates – although, since 2011, there has been a government-backed apprenticeship scheme in the UK. Graduates have degrees in a variety of subjects – and it is worth remembering that a good, creative agency will have staff with a wide range of backgrounds.

---

[107] http://wadds.co.uk/2012/11/18/public-relations-as-a-profession-applying -for-chartered-qualification/ (accessed March 6, 2013).

How to pay for PR services

How you pay for public relations affects how well an agency (or consultant) performs – whether they "sweatshop" the work, or do a proper job. Public relations is – in the definition I prefer to use – "the planned persuasion of people to behave in ways that further its sponsor's objectives".[108] The words "planned persuasion" are important, because they indicate that a public relations practitioner is not a mere spammer of press releases, but is bringing valuable expertise about how to communicate a company's messages.

This is why payment to an agency is normally in the form of a professional fee, either a fixed sum for a project, an agreed retainer or a daily or hourly rate. There are some crude pay-by-clipping services, which are sometimes offered by marketing companies. Here, the incentives are wrong.

The agency may call it "payment by results" (PBR). But the clients who want this service invariably provide neither money nor margin to pay for any proper evaluation, so it really is normally just payment for cuttings. The result, all too often, is low-grade, sweatshop-produced publicity, which does not utilise any creativity, and fails to inspire readers or deliver real business objectives.

The model encourages the vendors to sign up as many PR clients as possible, without appropriately increasing their staff

---

[108] Trevor Morris and Simon Goldsworthy, *PR: A Persuasive Industry? Spin, Public Relations and the Shaping of the Modern Media* (London: Palgrave Macmillan, 2008), p. 102.

numbers, and then go after the lowest-hanging fruit with quickly-drafted press statements, which are spammed to hundreds of journalists. The clients for whom the easiest coverage can be found will be prioritised.

You may recall, back in Chapter 1, that I referred to audits of executives who fund PR activities. They did not, it turned out, see coverage as the goal. The execs wanted easily measurable results, such as how effective PR activity has been at (a) raising awareness and (b) delivering key messages to the target audience. An agency that is charging you by counting any old clippings is missing the point. And, let's face it, if an agency is just doing the easy stuff, it makes outsourcing the work to them rather pointless.

Moreover, journalists hate the idea that a PR company charges a fixed rate for a mention in their articles. Alexia Tsotsis, co-editor of TechCrunch, a popular AOL-owned website, was scathing about this arrangement:[109]

While we're not in the business of advising PR people on their pricing, we think that making press coverage this transactional crosses an ethical/editorial line and diminishes the integrity of our brand and our writers . . . We will be banning . . . anyone who we catch doing this from pitching [to] us. . . .

The view is echoed by Martin Bryant, Managing Editor of The Next Web, who says: "In truth, if I knew how much a PR firm

[109] http://techcrunch.com/2012/11/08/we-are-worth-at-least-3k/ (accessed March 5, 2013).

charges when I publish a post about one of their clients, I'd feel a bit dirty."[110]

In practice, hiring a PR agency is about hiring their staff's time, just as much as if you hire an in-house staff member. If they are paid for their time, they are incentivised to be helpful to you regardless of whether an activity will result in cuttings. They will be keen to invest their time in difficult-to-secure, but well-worth-it coverage in the most prestigious, best-read titles. This work might include, for example, having meetings with journalists – something that the pay-for-cuttings brigade won't necessarily wish to do.

Above all, a good PR practitioner will sometimes advise you not to try to get press coverage, when the results would not be in your interests. One company asked me if I would get them featured in the investigative magazine *Private Eye*. My advice was not to seek this coverage, because, in this case, it seemed to me that there was significant risk that the magazine might instinctively support the other side. Would an agency that relies on cuttings for its income give the same advice?

---

[110] http://thenextweb.com/media/2012/11/09/i-dont-want-to-know-how
-much-we-are-worth/ (accessed March 5, 2013).

Chapter 10

Future Learning

The PR world – just like every industry – has two types of people in it. There are those who are constantly learning, who hunger after new techniques and keep up to date with the latest thinking. And then there are those who don't, who think they know everything – but are actually a little bit rubbish at their jobs. If you're reading this book then you are, by definition – thank goodness – one of the former.

It may seem strange for someone who has written a book called *The PR Masterclass* to admit to this, but I go to all sorts of people's training workshops, and to breakfast briefings about well-run PR campaigns. I read lots of books on the industry too, and on PR's colourful historical figures, many of whom ran fascinating but long-forgotten campaigns. I am not alone in doing this. When I left the national press and started doing PR training workshops, I was initially amazed at some of the experienced and high-profile people who booked. "Why on earth does such-and-such want training?", I asked myself. But I quickly realised that these people are experienced and successful precisely because they always want to find out new ways of getting better results.

The best PR teams ensure that there is a learning culture at their core. We know that countries that are open to globalisation grow faster than those which close themselves off from the world.[111] Just look at North Korea. Similarly, those PR practitioners who engage with others in the industry and the thinking that others develop are likely to do better. Those who shut themselves off are likely to stagnate. Therefore I would encourage everyone – whether in-house, at an agency, or freelance – to join a well-run trade or professional body. This will help you to interact with other good practitioners, and learn about innovative PR campaigns. In the UK, the rapidly growing PRCA runs breakfast time sessions in which successful campaigns are explained, plus member drinks events – all invaluable opportunities for getting information that will help your PR activities.

Many of the good agencies regularly run training afternoons, where they bring outside experts to speak. Others allocate money per head for every staff member to go on external courses. Since quitting journalism, I have found myself training in-house teams at companies from Kellogg's to Axa, and many of the biggest and best agencies. A sizeable number in our industry have a hunger to stay at the top of the game. Before this book draws to a close, let's look at some of the resources that can help.

The essential reading list

One of the best books I read in 2012 was *Rethinking Reputation: How PR Trumps Marketing and Advertising in the New Media World*. It's by two American authors, Fraser P. Seitel and John Doorley, and is a sensible, easy-to-read guide on managing a reputation and on crisis communication.

---

[111] Greg Mankiw, http://gregmankiw.blogspot.co.uk/2006/04/measuring-effects -of-globalization.html (accessed March 5, 20130).

I mentioned *Crisis Management: Planning for the Inevitable* by Steven Fink earlier in the book. I have read most books out there on crisis communications, and most are tediously academic. This one is heart felt and practical, because the author was personally involved during the Three Mile Island nuclear disaster, when he served on the Pennsylvania Governor's crisis management team. He has subsequently written a follow-up book called *Crisis Communications: The Definitive Guide to Managing the Message*, which I also recommend.

PR: A Persuasive Industry? Spin, Public Relations and the Shaping of the Modern Media, by Trevor Morris and Simon Goldsworthy, is a useful guide to how public relations works, and is eminently realistic in its outlook. They authors don't hold by the more outlandish claims of the PR chatterati, which is unsurprising given that one-half of the writing team spent most of his career in agencies, rather than just writing about them.

Mark Weiner's *Unleashing the Power of PR* is a challenge to the PR industry to carry out its measurement and evaluation better. The author has worked since 1994 implementing evaluation systems for public relations, so the book is not just theoretical, but full of practical advice and examples.

Steve Harrison's biography of Howard Gossage, *Changing the World is the Only Fit Work for a Grown Man*, examines one practitioner who fused advertising and public relations. Harrison's book covers his most famous campaigns, techniques from which can usefully be copied today.

Share This: The Social Media Handbook for PR Professionals brings together a group of 24 leading UK practitioners who are part of the social media panel of the Chartered Institute of Public Relations. It has become a handbook of best practice and the latest thinking.

The Social Media MBA, edited by Christer Holloman, uses case studies from companies such as Dell and Kodak to show ways to reap bigger rewards from social media than the obvious ones.

My Trade: A Short History of British Journalism by Andrew Marr gives an inside view of how the British press works, from a former newspaper editor and one of the BBC's top talkshow presenters.

Useful websites

Reading *PRWeek* (prweek.com in the UK and prweekus.com in the US) is a great way of keeping up with industry trends. There are excellent online magazines, *The Drum* (thedrum.com), Mark Ragan's *PR Daily* (prdaily.com), *The Holmes Report* (holmesreport. com) and *PRMoment* (prmoment.com). In the UK, *Communicate* (communicatemagazine.co.uk) and *CorpComms* (corpcomms-magazine.co.uk) are well-respected subscription magazines, while, in the USA, *O'Dwyer's* (www.odwyerpr.com) is a lively, even compulsive, read.

Behind the Spin (www.behindthespin.com) is a guide for students to the PR world. It has published interviews with industry heavyweights and useful information about courses.

Meanwhile, Twitter is an effective way of keeping up with the thinking of other figures in the PR industry, including many agency heads. I come across a lot of interesting research this way.

The future

If you get some interesting results from implementing the techniques in book, why not drop me a line and let me know about them? I'm at book@alexsingleton.com and normally reply personally within a day. Finally, if you register your book at www.alexsingleton.com/register, I'll send you some exclusive bonus materials, including three videos that further illustrate the techniques in this book.

ABOUT THE AUTHOR

Alex Singleton is one of the world's leading public relations strate-gists. Through consultancy, training and speaking, he helps organ-isations, large and small, all over the world. Companies such as Kellogg's, Virgin Atlantic and FirstGroup, along with major chari-ties and public bodies, have turned to him for his expertise.

Alex was previously a journalist at *The Daily Telegraph* in London and has also written for *The Guardian*, the *Daily Express* and *Mail Online*. He has been interviewed on countless news programmes on broadcasters such as the BBC, CNN, CNBC and Bloomberg, and successfully appeared on Channel Four's comedy show *Ten O'Clock Live*.

He ran PR campaigns as Research Director of the Adam Smith Institute and President of the Globalisation Institute, and has given testimony in House of Commons and House of Lords select committees.

ACKNOWLEDGEMENTS

Sorry, but you've come to the self-indulgent part of the book. I hope this isn't too tedious. But stick with me – you get a mention.

I've always warmed to people whose default behaviour is to encourage. And I'd never have been in a position to write this book without them. Mark Moxon, a magazine editor, gave me my first break. He had the immense wisdom or insanity to give me, then a schoolboy, a monthly column in a computing magazine. This gave me my first appearance on the shelves of WHSmith – and a thorough education in magazine publishing.

I worked with countless brilliant and professional writers and editors at *The Telegraph*, but here I'll just name four who were immensely helpful: Iain Martin and Simon Heffer, who saw my potential, Will Lewis, who was responsible for my being hired, and Damian Thompson, a fantastic columnist and great conversationalist, who forced me to write better.

This book would never have happened without the enthusiasm of my agent, Anthony Haynes, who instantly saw its potential and was relentless. I couldn't have wished for a better publishing team than Jonathan Shipley, Jenny Ng, Vicky Kinsman and Carly Hounsome at Wiley, who, with their colleagues, are responsible for this book being in your hands now.

And, lastly, let me thank you for choosing this book. I'm always happy to hear from those like you who are considering implementing the ideas in this book, so you are very welcome to contact me at book@alexsingleton.com. I read messages sent to that address personally and normally respond.

INDEX